SPIRITUAL – Faith…
Where's It? I Need It!

By

APOSTLE PAULP

For permission requests, write to **USA Writers and Publishers**

support@usawritersandpublishers.com
www.usawritersandpublishers.com

Printed and published in the United States of America.

TABLE OF CONTENTS

Introduction

This book on **Faith** welcomes you all on board as our **Flight on Faith** takes off.

Our flight will be for **sixty (60) minutes**, and our **Pilot — the Lord God Almighty —** promises there will be **turbulent weather**, but we are to be reassured that our **Flight of Faith** will reach its destination **on time and safely**.

On behalf of our **hostess — Grace, Mercy, and Peace —** and myself, a **great welcome!**

As soon as we reach our **100,000 feet altitude**, we will be serving a **spiritual menu**. Please, keep your **safety belts fastened** and your **window blinds open at all times**, to prevent **doubt, discouragement, and dismay**, who may try to get a **free flight with us!**

So, sit back, relax, and enjoy our **Flight to Faith**, dear passengers.

And please note — all seats are **free**, with **no first class or second class**, and **no front or rear seats** — for in this flight, **we are all equal before God!**

T.O.P. — TRUST, OBEDIENCE, and PROVISION

The By-products of FAITH... and the Path to the TOP.

Chapter 1

IN GENESIS 3:15

God says, **"I will put enmity (the state or feeling of being opposed or hostile to someone) between thee and the woman, and (then) between thy (man) seed and her (woman) seed — it shall (will) bruise thy (who?) head, and thou shalt bruise his head."**

This is **immediate authority given over the spirit of darkness!**

While **James 4:4** exposes the action of rooted hate between the world and God, in the **carnal mind (Romans 8:7)**, it is vexed with God and creates animosity and hostility.

In the **Book of Genesis**, there is full of original evidence of gifts given to men, and **faith is one of them**. God's faith came to redeem mankind at the birth of sin, and then everything followed. God only came to redeem us who were born in sin.

Wow! What a man of faith! Who sinned? Adam. But He, God, came to and for us, and gave Adam's repentance, and gave Adam's redemption.

God had faith for one man — and what did He, God, do 2000 years ago? He came again, not for just one Adam but billions of us, and offered us **total redemption!**

It's a very high level of trust, love, faith, and compassion. Yes, He came not just for Israel, His nation, but unto and for all of us. **Hallelujah!**

And God's faith, trust in us grew, that He not only gave us Adam but also gave us Eve, and gave us the right to multiply and bring forth His seed through us. **Hallelujah!**

What manner of faith planted in and through us!

And look what God did — gave full exposure of faith in Adam to name the animals, not just on land but in the wide ocean!

What was Adam's peripheral vision? Where did Adam go to school to learn — and if he did, who taught him?

Philippians 2:5 states, *"Let this mind, of God, be in us, which is also in Christ Jesus."* Let us note here again — He is referred to as **Christ Jesus** vs. **Jesus Christ. Why?**

The strength God gives to mankind comes through faith, and **without faith it is impossible to please Him!**

And Paul, an Apostle of God, urged us as Christians to not only have faith but to use it — as **faith without works is dead!**

So, let us go to **Ephesians 3**, stopping at verse 17, where it states: *"That Christ, the Lord Jesus Christ, will — not maybe, but will —*

dwell, reside, abide in my heart, your heart, and in our heart by faith, not our thought, not what we are led to think."

Because the same chapter, verse 20, reassures us:
"Now unto Him, God, that is to do, and will do exceedingly (continue chapter one) abundantly above all — not some — that we ask or think, according to His power that works in all of us."

Amen!

We need to activate this imposed strength. We must believe it, just as you believe the water you drink went to your stomach — as easy as that!

We go to the gym to increase our muscles, yes? Do likewise when we read His Word — that is called **fellowship!**

He invites us into **"courtship" (Psalm 100:4)** — *Enter His gates, His house, His presence!*

Behold, in His presence, and when I looked up, a voice said unto me, **"Be not afraid: remember Me, your Lord, I am great, I am terrible, and I fight for you — My sons, My daughters, My wives, and My houses."**

And God brought their victory to nought. **Amen!**

Remember Nehemiah — a great leader — had the big job of rebuilding the walls of Jerusalem. He was up against terrible opposition, but that did not deter him. He was plugged into his **faith socket**.

God allowed him, Nehemiah, to show the power of his faith that God hath given him.

How do we get our **license?** We drive for it!

Seeds we sow must bring a **harvest.**

IT IS VERY IMPORTANT THAT WE AS CHILDREN OF GOD

(Not Christians), must learn that it is **not healing that breeds faith**, but it is **faith that brings healing.**

Let us look at the proof of this — the woman who touched the hem of Jesus' garment — she was healed without Jesus identifying her or praying.

The man by the pool for **30 years**, the Lord Jesus Christ asked, "Do you want to be healed?"

Did Lazarus have faith? **Yes!** And so did the Lord Jesus Christ — so He called a dead man.

Lazarus (Mary's brother, who had anointed the Lord) was in the grave for **four days**, not three, and the body had begun to show decay and expose odor.

Martha went to meet the Lord Jesus Christ and filed her complaint, just like any wife would do. But she had a **huge deposit of faith**, and that which is delayed will never be denied.

(Acts 17:28)
"For in Him we live, and move, and have our being; for we are (also) His offspring."

The keyword here is **"also."**
That means there must be other "offsprings." And who are they???

(Acts 17:29) says,
"Forasmuch as we are the offspring of God, we are not to think that the Godhead is like unto gold, silver, or stone."

(John 18:37)
"...For this cause I came into the world, that I should bear witness unto the truth. So, everyone that is of the truth heareth my voice."

(Note: "heareth my voice" — big difference! This is how close we need to be — that is, in a relationship.)

In the Gospels, our Lord Jesus Christ refers to Himself as **Son of Man** eighty (80) times. **Why?**

Rockets after early take-off (60–90 minutes), it releases a heavy portion of its weight at a certain altitude. **Why?**

We are to **lay aside the things (weight), sins that so easily beset us**, and **run, walk, drive** (Hebrews 12:1).

Procrastination, disobedience, slow motion — these are the **weights** we are to get rid of so **faith will come and reside in us**.

Please do not miss it — **GOD has (past tense) given us our faith from day one!**

Jeremiah, a teenager, was assigned to ministry, but **Jeremiah tried to refuse his assignment**. He was looking at what? **His age.**
While GOD was looking at what? **His heart!**

It is out of the **abundance of the heart** our **mouth speaks**, **Hallelujah!**

How much am I to hold on to **Faith — God's unchanging hand**?
I am to **never let Mercy** nor **Truth** ever forsake me or us. Instead, I lift my plea and call out:

"Lord, Lord, bind us totally and write it plainly on the tablets of our hearts."

For I must first **see**, then **become the witness** to the world around me — **Hallelujah!**

I am to show His **fullness** — His **Faith** — buried deep within me, within us, and to **enjoy the spoils of this Faith** that lives in us. This Faith brings glory **not to those around us** — friends, family, or enemies — **but to God Himself.**

Just as God used **Abraham**, **Mary**, and **Joseph**, their lives were not mere words — they were living **evidence of trust, proof of Faith** in God, not in man, not in pastor, but in **God alone!**

We are to **show it**, not just tell it — **Hallelujah!**

We must understand **every word** God speaks to us, for out of this understanding, **Faith gives birth to the weapon we are to use completely — Faith itself!**

Our **mustard seed**, though small (just 1–2 millimeters in diameter, yellowish-white to black), stands as the **symbol of Faith** in the New Testament. Yet that tiny seed grows into a **large tree**, where even **birds love to perch in** — not on — its branches.

When **ground and mixed** with water or vinegar, it produces a strong, vibrant **mustard** — just like how **our tested Faith** releases its strength and flavor into our lives.

That is the **power of Faith** — small in appearance, mighty in purpose!

FAITH *(Hebrew: Emunah)* — means *trust, rely, to be persuaded.*

OH, HALLILUJAH IT IS OUR SPIRITUAL MUSTLE, THAT CAN AND WILL LIFT ANYTHING, HALLILUJAH!
And in **Greek**, *Pistis* means *faith, trust, fides, steadfastness, firmness* (**Exodus 17:12**).

Faith is inspired (**breathed out**) by God through the Holy Spirit in us (**Romans 10:17**).

Jesus is the Pioneer, Captain, and Prince of Faith, which ultimately comes from God by *hearing*—and *hearing through the Word of God* through the Holy Spirit.

FAITH — IS IT A NOUN (person, place, or thing) OR A VERB (action)?

ACTION, WORKS — if we do not have the verb, action is dead! And without faith? We will never please God!!!

Great Commission — that's what faith is: an exhibition, a witness all over — Jerusalem, Judea, Samaria, unto the uttermost part of this earth — through the faith generator.

Look at the ninth hour *(Acts 10:4)* when to Cornelius, the angel appearing said, "Thy prayers and thy alms are come up for a memorial before God." Our prayers are based upon our faith and the level it's at. It starts at a mustard-seed level but grows into this large tree!

Let's look over to Peter and his Great Commission when he was on the housetop (at the sixth hour) and "saw the heavens opened, and a certain vessel descending unto who?" Him — Peter.

Where have we placed our faith — covered?

It reminds me of two things I didn't have: money and faith! And thirty miles away from home, with the gas needle on empty! But I suddenly saw that same needle move — not to a full tank, but to about a quarter — and I was home. Oh, it was not midday; it was closer to midnight!!!!

A very important point here, very important — I did not rush to church and give a testimony, not for over five years. Why? Glad you asked!

God saw my faith level was even lower than my gas tank — a huge problem — so He gave me the result of what faith will and can do, so I am taught.

So just as we have the automobile accelerator...

FAITH IS WHAT GIVES US PROTECTION

Faith — what is it really? **Who gives it? What sustains it? When does it come alive?**
We often ask: does it come from wisdom? From knowledge? From understanding?

Faith is more than all these things — and yes, it **comes with a cost.** That cost may be **monetary, mental, spiritual, marital, or even parental.**

When the clouds are full, they empty themselves upon the earth (Ecclesiastes 11:3).
So too, when faith fills our hearts, it must pour out into every part of our lives.

In **Judges 1:1**, we see that the people sought God before they moved forward.

In **2 Chronicles 7:14**, He calls His people to humble themselves, pray, seek His face, and turn from wicked ways — for only then will He heal the land.
In **Isaiah 46:9**, He reminds us, *"I am God, and there is none like Me."*

And in **Acts 16:24–31**, we find Paul and Silas — beaten, chained, and imprisoned — yet **praying and singing hymns** in the darkness.
What were they using to pray with?
You guessed it — **Faith!**

Blessings already exist in the spiritual realm, but it is **prayer that births them on earth.**
Faith is built within us, programmed into our very being, through the **relationship** — the **divine marriage** — between God and us.

Behold, the Lord says, *"I come in."*
Where does He enter?
Through the **front door** of our lives — into our **living room**, our **dining table** — the everyday places where we live, eat, and breathe.

He sits with us. He drinks from our cup.
Why? To prove the birth of a relationship.

It doesn't matter what's in that cup — water, wine, or tears — because God is **planting a faith-garden** within us.

He brings garments of faith for us to wear — the **helmet of salvation**, the **lamp unto our feet**, the **armor of righteousness**. We are **fully dressed in the adornment of faith.**

Why would He do this?
Because everything God preaches, He also **embodies.**
And just as He aligns Himself with the Father, He assigns that same manifestation **through us**, that we may serve as witnesses.

So, we are **armed for spiritual CPR —**
Christ Restores & Protects.

It is by His grace that we are saved,
but it is **through His faith** planted within us that we live.
For without faith, it is impossible to please God —
not tithes, not church attendance, not outward rituals —
but faith, the inward trust that aligns us with His Word.

Inside the tabernacle, when the Word is preached and received, we grasp hold of **His righteousness.**
This gives us reassurance and restores the image of God within us.

Yet many of us keep searching for something we already have — unaware that we even **need** what's already been **given!**

"Blessed shalt thou be when thou comest in, and blessed shalt thou be when thou goest out" (Deuteronomy 28:6).
The gates of hell **shall not prevail** against us.

We are told to **decree a thing**, and it shall be established.
Life and death are in the power of the tongue.

We were created in His likeness, just as Adam and Eve were.
And John declared, *"There is One who comes after me, whose shoelace I am not worthy to untie."*
Who is that one? Jesus.
But do you see the mystery here?
He also spoke of **us**, His body, who would continue His work upon the earth.

Jesus said, *"Not even Solomon, in all his wisdom, can compare with you, the children of God."*

The human mind thinks over **forty thousand times a day.**
But imagine enclosing every one of those thoughts in **faith.**
How different would our lives be?

Take a moment and do a self-evaluation.

How many things do you think about in an hour?

Write it down — reflect, and see how often your thoughts turn to fear instead of faith.

Trust in the Lord with all your heart and lean not on your own understanding.

To "stand under" His Word means to be **covered** by it —

like standing in the rain, completely soaked in His presence.

When Peter went back to the deep to cast his net again, he didn't just obey — he Dived **into the depth of faith.**

That's what God is calling us to do:

To dive deep, be soaked, be filled, and live out the greatest gift of all — **FAITH.**

FAITH IS OUR CREDIT CARD

Faith is **OUR CREDIT CARD** (God gives a 950-credit score), not a debit card (as with DC we owe).

Faith — we are to use it! Don't stop! Do we pray without stopping?

PUSH – Pray Until Something Happens

BUSH – Believe Until Something Happens

Is my faith like a long-distance call or an ordinary local call?

He will move mountains or allow us to climb our mountains from right where we are now — *"We fear no evil."*

We Christians, children of God, are subject to **persecutions** — spiritual attack, spiritual confrontations, disappointments, disarray, discomfort (physical, mental).

We are **qualified for persecutions** because of righteousness living in us — and that righteousness is not of us but of **The Lord God Almighty.**

And the devil knows the difference… he asked The Lord Jesus Christ, *"If thou be the Son of God, jump from this building."*

What is very important here is **why** the devil (spirit of darkness) challenges God to jump. Is this same confrontation we are challenged with? But why?

The spirit knows about our faith and knows how to measure it clearly!

Did he say, *"Peter, I know?"*
"James, I know?"
Did he not say, *"Mary, I know?"*

Their faith-tank was not just full, but **overflowing!**

We ask ourselves — **is my faith door locked? Shut? Or closed?**

Our God knows **when to open doors**, and **He knows when to close them**.
It is for us to know **when to enter** and **when to close.**

Be careful — as most doors **swing both ways.**
Be **very careful**, our **faith-door** swings **one way only!**

Faith's **first manifestation** came with and through **Adam's creation.**
In **Genesis 1:26**, God said, *"Let Us make man in Our image, after Our likeness."*
At that very moment, **faith was transferred** — from the Creator to His creation.

God made **Adam** just like Himself, and then made **Eve** to be like Adam.
This divine act extended faith to both — a **shared inheritance** of God's nature and trust.

But then came **Genesis 3:24** — the separation.
Did Adam shut his **faith door**?
Yes, he did.
But did God do likewise?
No!

Even after the fall, **God's faith in His creation remained.**
He still believed in the potential of His likeness in man —
and through that faith, **the plan of redemption began.**

We are going to **Exodus 17:12** for the **first mention of faith.**
Where **faith**, in Hebrew, is *Emunah* — and in Greek, *Pistis* — and with an English interpretation as:
Trust, Fides, Amen, Rely, Firmness, Steadfastness, Fidelity.

Children of God (COG) — all we have to do is simply choose one of those and tie it to the area of our life that we will "prescribe" for "healing."

E.g. **Steadfastness!** Wow!
This is bringing out the fruit of faith that makes us show how resolute or dutiful, how firm and unwavering we are — **armed against adversity.**
Yes, we are!

When the cop stops us, we show what?
Our **ID.**
So, when we are stopped by the spirit of darkness, what ID do we pull out?

God is always able to trust you because He sees and knows who and what is planted in us — by the fruits, firmness, and trust.

Do we see God recognizes Abraham's faith as righteousness — by the trust and belief Abraham has in God?
So, it is very evident that our faith is totally in God — not our husband, or wife, or our pastor, VIP!

Yes, I know that our level of faith is the traffic on a four-lane highway: one going at 90 mph, another 75 mph, another 65, and the fourth going at 45!

It is how we live our Christian life.

We determine how much we press our faith "accelerator," when God pre-made our life with a speed of 100!

We set our own limits, which slow down the time we take to reap our rewards set awaiting us!

How many of us, "driving" on God's highway, are looking out for "limits," when God did not put any there?

We "look out" for the "state troopers" when God has removed them long ago.

Do we forget whose "road" we're driving on?

TRAINING IN FAITH

Remember, I have to train you… My child, remember I have to train you all before you go!

This is not about a physical "go," but a **spiritual go!**

Because, my child (My children), just like how you/we have to start our "aeroplane,"

we all have to **switch on our faith-engine,** the same way God asked of Adam in the Garden:

"Who gave you Eve?"

Someone you did not ask for — but God saw Adam's heart and "planted" a garden in his heart that brought forth?
You got it — **Eve!!**

So right now, wherever you are, visit your heart and see what it's telling your mind that you want or need.
Go ahead!!!
And make a note of that thought — write it down and see what becomes of it in seven days!

Watch the result — what is it?
(0%? or 100%?) **Amen!**

FAITH BUILT ON HOPE

Faith is built on **hope**, **wish**, then you will get the visit of **manifestation** that has been planted long ago.
So He says to **Jeremiah**, so says He also to us:

"Before you were conceived in your mother's womb, I, your God, knew (past tense) you."

Turn your thoughts over to **Jabez**, which means *Poverty*.
But Jabez (means Poverty) knew that meaning — did he accept it?
Never did!!!

He went outside where his faith sent him and looked at all the lands that belonged to him.

Wow!

FAITH IN ACTION

How long have you been living in "the pit"?
Five years? Five months?
Are we taking up full-time residence there?

Moses came upon the Red Sea with the children of Israel and the king's army behind.
But make a spiritual stop and…

"What have you in your hand, Moses?"

God will always check us out mentally before we show where our faith is!

What state are you now, as against Moses then?
Press on your **faith-accelerator** and head on to your **faith-highway** — it has no stop signs, none!

If you see your **odometer** showing under 100 mph?
Press! Press! And get back up there!

Moses took back up his rod — let's do the same!

A TESTIMONY OF FAITH

I remember going to my bank for a loan, after praying for someone — not about my loan.

I went to the bank shortly after, and my manager said,

"Paul, I am busy. Go to Mr. David and tell him to give you whatever you ask for."

So, when our Lord says, "Before we open our mouth, He will bless," let us try getting "reading glasses" to see our answers — **look to Him at our faith.**

FAITH COMPARED

We should also look at **Joshua.**

Faith... is your **pipe water** that we turn off.
Even though water is there? Yes?

Or our **light switch** is turned off? Yes?
But current (220 volts) is in our "line."

Also, our **radio** is not playing? Yes?
But is it turned on?
And if so, on what station is it on? **Praise and exhortation?**

Please remind ourselves — it's God's faithfulness that fills us up, cultivates, and plants faith in us!!!!

for flow and clarity.

THE OUTER EXHIBITION OF FAITH

The **outer exhibition of faith** we are looking at now is referred to as **phototropic**, which exposes us to **light**, just as the tree comes out to light in a range of terrestrial and aquatic environments. It reduces the CO_2 and builds **oxygen**, *Amen!*

It says in:

John 1:2 – *"The same was in the beginning with God."*
John 8:12 – *"Then spake Jesus again unto them, saying, I am the light of the world: he that followeth Me shall not walk in darkness but shall have the light of life."*
Psalm 1:3 – *"Our leaves shall not wither but bring forth our/His fruit in our/His season."*

Let us **bridge** the two — the **gravitropic** and the **phototropic** — which form **bidirectional spiritual growth**.
While we are still human, it exposes exactly who we are — not only in God's sight but to the whole wide world.

This image must always **show in us and through us**, shining that **large beam of light wherever we go**, by the life we live.
Amen!

Our minds must never "look behind," as our instructions are:

"Look unto Him, the Author and Finisher of our life."

We are *His image* and *His righteousness*, landed here on earth in the image of *"Greater than Solomon."*
A **crown of righteousness** is afforded unto us!

Jeremiah's Example

The people of Judah were **Jeremiah's own people** — yes, his own people (just like Judas, just like Peter) — who **dig the pit** for our fall.

But what of the faith God gives us in **Romans 12**?
It's time to **put it in gear!**

Jeremiah had his **thoughts**, not God's.
His excuse was, *"I am a child."*

He, Jeremiah, used this out of his own knowledge — what he saw — and tried to **disqualify himself!**
Wow!!!

Not realizing that's not who God saw.

What God saw was **who He, God, had created** — just like Job, just like David, just like... yes, **you!**

And this stop is just a **pit stop** — a 60-second pit stop to **recharge for the road to victory** — and your **faith tank is full!**

How many times are we reminded by this?

"For I know the thoughts that I think toward you," saith the Lord, *"to give you an expected end."* — **Jeremiah 29:11**

Now, replace *Jeremiah* and say:

"John, Mary, Peter, Sharon, Michael, Beverly," and so on!

Prophesy to yourself just as Jesus did and kept doing to teenager Jeremiah!

Note — Jeremiah said he was a child and used that to disqualify himself, yes?
Correct.

But Jesus did not see him, Jeremiah, that way!
God saw him as a *child of God!*

That "**of God**" makes a huge difference!

Faith in Action

Let's go back to **Jabez**, who was born in poverty.
But was that to be his life?
No!

The **Hebrew boys** were in the fire — but what?
Burned to death?
No!!!

Ask yourself that question.

God reminds us: before we open our mouth, He **will answer**!

It is that **walk in faith** that leads us into those answers awaiting us.

Restaurants do what? **Pre-prepare** the menu.
Why? To **reduce waiting time** — like in **Isaiah 65:24**:

"Before they call, I will answer; and while they are still speaking, I the Lord will hear."

I want to speak to my wife — I call her.
I want to talk to my bank — I call them.
So, when I want to talk to **my God**, I talk to Him.
But how?

Do I have faith? Because if I have no faith, I **cannot please God!**

That is what **Hebrews 11:6** says:

"Without faith it is impossible to please God."

And who knows that more than me!

I prayed morning, noon, and night — Saturday, Tuesday — fasted, went to Pastor (even though I was one), prayed for five days, twelve days, burned candles, put up my water glasses — you name it!

No answer! None!

But as I **repented** — not with any Pastor, not with any Apostle, but by myself — and **walked away**, a level of **restoration overtook me** in my health and finances, better than before, **just like Job!**

(A joyful wordplay on living flavorfully in His presence!)

"We must be able to identify our pitfalls, different from our pitstops!"

(Jeremiah 1:5) — "Before I, the LORD, formed and created thee in the womb, I knew (not *know*) thee; and before thou camest forth out of the womb, I sanctified thee (approved) and ordained thee (charged with holy orders) — just as I came in Mary's womb!"

When was Jeremiah called a prophet unto the nations? How long did Jeremiah have to labor? Did we realize that Jeremiah had **two wombs**?

(Luke 12:32) — "Fear not, my little flock, for it is your Father's pleasure to give you, my Kingdom."

Trust Me — I give you My only Son *(Romans 8:32)* — delivered Him up for you all, and I freely give unto you, My children, **all things... all things!**

So, let us turn on our **"Faith Switch"** and see the **fullness of My faith** planted within you!

FAITH

"Trust in Me." — Is this a command? Yes! For we are not to lean on our **own understanding**, but in **all** our ways — not some — we are to **acknowledge Him** through **FAITH**.

It's not a *commandment*; it is a **command** — a call to total trust. For without FAITH, we **cannot please Him**.

Listen! It is **God Himself** who comes to your door and **knocks**.
But **why** does He knock?
Because love never forces its way in — it waits to be invited.
Faith is that open door.

FAITH is from the Hebrew word **EMNAH**, which means **TO TAKE A FIRM ACTION, A REASSURED ACTION, AN ACTION WITHOUT ANY EVIDENCE OF DOUBT.** We place our **Trust, reliance upon, and IN GOD** — our **Belief** and **Confidence** in a higher Power, the Spiritual Force, or the religious teaching — and our **Conviction** in something without physical evidence or Proof. It is more about **knowing HIM** than doing things.

FAITH is the **Loyalty or Allegiance** to the Lord God Almighty through instructions and Principles.

TYPES OF FAITH:

1. **RELIGIOUS** – Based on spiritual or theological beliefs.
2. **PERSONAL** – Trust in oneself, our abilities, or life's purpose.
3. **INTERPERSONAL** – Trust and loyalty in relationships.

FAITH gives the benefit of **EMOTIONAL COMFORT and PEACE, PURPOSE and MEANING, RESILIENCE and STRENGTH, GUIDANCE and DIRECTION**, and **COMMUNITY and BELONGING**.

What is it to **LAY OUR BURDENS DOWN, GET RID OF THEM ALL**, and then **PICK UP FAITH, RECEIVE FAITH, ACTIVATE FAITH!**

Let me take you with me on our **FAITH-ISSUE**. Let us go to the **SUPERMARKET** with our **CREDIT CARD**. We are going to stay here for about **70 minutes** and pick up what we need. We will always pick up according to our desire and the amount of dollars we can afford, VIP!

As we walk, I see flour with different amounts, different brands, and of course, different prices. And now I am going to the cashier and pull out my credit card and am told my total is **$597.67!** I insert my card and get my receipt—**Amen!**

All I am asking us (you) to do is picture this: walking into **God's Spiritual Supermarket** and doing the same. You are now standing at the cashier, and the bill you get is **$97.67!** A whopping **$97.67!** And your card got accepted—**Hallelujah!**

But did you notice the difference in the amount you spent in both "supermarkets"? A whopping **$500!** And I ask you, **why?** The answer is the **level of FAITH** we have in our daily life versus our spiritual life!

God will now pull us aside and say, *Peter, James, Yevonne,* **"I SEE NO LEVEL OF FAITH IN YOU, NONE!"**

Now we become despondent, hold our heads down, and begin to wonder—what is it? And the Spirit of God calls us aside and says:

Romans 12:3 – *"I have given you your own measure of faith!"*

Go and use it, so I will be pleased with you, **My Child!**

Chapter 2

Let us measure: **how far am I from my faith?**

Look at water — it is hot at 211 degrees, but begins boiling when? At 212 degrees! Only **1 degree** from boiling. It is the same with our faith!

We have to be reassured — it is alive in us. Just like the child in a mother's womb, very much alive, so too is our FAITH impregnated by God in Us, Hallelujah!

Hebrews 11:1 says,

"Now faith, not tomorrow's, is being totally sure of our hopes for and be totally sure of what our natural eyes do not and can never see."

1 Samuel 1:1 speaks of two wives of the same husband. One was a mother, and the other could not become one, as the Lord had shut up her womb. Who did? Yes, **the Lord!**

And her husband, Elkanah, asked his wife,

"Is not all ten sons good enough for you?"

In verse fifteen, **Hannah said,**

"I am a woman of sorrowful spirit, and I have poured out my soul unto the Lord."

Hannah finally conceived and brought forth who? **Samuel!**

Here, Hannah not only conceived but gave total honor and reverence by not going up until the child was weaned. And she, Hannah, gave her child back unto the Lord.

We will develop a **season** — a winter, a spring, an autumn, or a summer.
But faith does not come that way.

Who knows who? Do you know faith, or faith knows you?

Your hands are not short that you will not, you cannot reach me/us; neither your eye not closed that you cannot see me/us; neither are we far away from you that you will not, cannot reach or throw your shadow over us, as you did with (???) with your shadow.

Release this marriage as what is ordered by you — as to what it is (to be): **real, sincere, committed,** and facilitate us to reap the fruits of our **marriage-tree.**

We pray; we beseech the Father!

PROVERBS 10:22 says, *"The blessing of our Lord maketh rich, and He, God, addeth no sorrow with it."*

So, are we seeing any sorrow? Am I having any sorrow?

Proverbs 10:24 ... *"The desires of the righteous will be granted."* And *"The way of our Lord is to strengthen us, the upright."*

Proverbs 10:13 ... *"But he that is faithful in spirit concealeth the matter."*

Romans 8:32 ... *"How shall He not with Him also freely give us all things?"*
And verse 35 in chapter 10 asks, *"Who or what shall/will separate us from the love of Christ?"*

So, if we are not separated, and we cannot be separated, we are living just as He, the Lord Jesus Christ, lives—unless we choose to move out. And why should I?

Faith is our **spiritual umbrella** that protects us from both *rain and sun.*

Our faith is not built by going to church on Sundays, or by our tithes, or by going to church on Saturdays, but it is the **gift of the Holy Spirit** before we are conceived—just as He did to Jeremiah!

Proverbs 20:7 says, *"A faithful man is hard to find, but a just man walks in integrity: and his children are blessed after him."* Amen!

Chapter 13:22 clearly states that *"A good man leaveth an inheritance to his children's children."*

It is so relevant, as the Jews had many children, grandchildren, and great-grandchildren, both sons and daughters.

And in **Ecclesiastes 2:26** it says, *"God giveth to a man that is good in His sight wisdom, and knowledge, and joy."*

So, God gives this unto us, and we are to store and use it.

HOW AND WHEN DO I GET FAITH

We often tend to think that faith came **after** the resurrection of Jesus Christ — but faith was here long before that. It existed **thousands of years ago**, even in the days of Noah, when it revealed itself strong and true.

Noah was a righteous man whom God loved deeply. Yet God, in His divine wisdom, chose to **flood the earth He had created** — not only to destroy but also to preserve.

Yes! God gave Noah specific instructions: to **build an ark** to exact measurements and design.

But let's pause and ask ourselves:
Did Noah go to school for this? Did he study engineering or architecture?
Of course not!

What Noah had was **faith** — a faith so strong that it moved him to obedience, even when he had never seen rain before.

Now, here's another question to stir our thoughts:
Were there any fishes on board?

God's instructions were clear — **for every living creature**. His plan was detailed, intentional, and filled with purpose.

Faith didn't begin with the resurrection; it began with **belief in God's Word** — trusting what we cannot yet see and obeying even when we do not understand.

JESUS ASKED PETER, HIS CHIEF DISCIPLE, "DO YOU LOVE ME?"
OK, PETER, IF YOU DO, GIVE ME EVIDENCE — GO FEED MY SHEEP!

FAITH IS THE MATERIAL THAT IS BUILT BY OUR CONSCIENCE (CON-SIENCE) THROUGH OUR WORSHIP IN THE AREA OF GIVING. PAUL, IN HIS WRITING TO THE HEBREWS, WANTED TO GET THEM IN THE **HEBREWS 6:1** MOOD — UNTO PERFECTION!

PAUL WANTED THEM TO HAVE A GOOD CONSCIENCE, A PERFECT CONSCIENCE, OUT OF WHICH WE WILL BECOME WHO GOD IS PLEASED WITH — A CHEERFUL GIVER!

REMEMBER THAT FAITH WITHOUT WORKS???? IS "DEAD FAITH!!!" IN FACT, IT CANNOT BE FAITH IF THERE IS NO WORK — IT IS DEAD, D-E-A-D! NO LIFE!!!

FAITH IS GIVEN TO ABRAHAM. HOW DO I KNOW THAT? THERE WERE NO SCRIPTURES, SO WHERE DID ABRAHAM GET IT FROM? ABRAHAM BECAME A FATHER, YES, AT AGE 99, BECAUSE GOD WANTED A SON TO SEND TO MINISTRY.

DID GOD HAVE THE OPTION TO MAKE ANOTHER ABEL? SURE!!! GOD HAS FAITH IN HIS HANDS AND WANTS SOMEONE, NOT SOMEWHERE, TO PLANT IT — AND GOD CHOSE ABRAHAM. WHY? HE WAS QUALIFIED, AS GOD CREATED HIM IN HIS (GOD'S) LIKENESS, AND GOD WANTED IT TO MULTIPLY!

(**ROMANS 12**) "BY GIVING EACH MAN THEIR OWN MEASURE…"

SO, DID CAIN HAVE FAITH? DID ABEL HAVE FAITH? WERE THEY MADE IN GOD'S LIKENESS?

AGAIN, PETER — "CAST YOUR NET AGAIN." (**JOHN 21:6**) PETER ASKED, "WHY GOD? I DID THAT ALREADY AND GOT NOTHING!"

PETER WAS QUESTIONING THE WORDS HE HEARD INSTEAD OF THE ONE WHO SAID IT, AND THIS IS A COMMON THING AMONG US, YES?

(**LUKE 5:1–11**)
(**ROMANS 12:2**) "BE NOT CONFORMED (be like, restrict, limit, imitate) TO THIS WORLD, BUT BE TRANSFORMED (modified, converted) BY THE RENEWING OF OUR MIND, BY THE INDWELLING OF AND BY THE HOLY SPIRIT THAT RESIDES, LIVES IN US." AMEN!

THE SAME **ROMANS 12**, IN VERSE 3, SAYS —
FOR FAITH TO COME ALIVE, TO BECOME ACTIVE, FIRSTLY LET'S NOT THINK OF OURSELVES MORE WORTHY OR HIGHER THAN OUR BROTHERS OR SISTERS, BUT WE ARE TO USE SOBER, FAIR JUDGMENT OF BEING EQUAL IN OUR LORD'S SIGHT.

(**JEREMIAH 17:7; PSALM 91:1**)

WHAT ARE THE QUALIFICATIONS TO HAVE FAITH

Walking in purpose by making our pitfalls our pitstops...

Faith allows me to answer. Faith allows me to identify my stops. The pitstops are short, and God refreshed Jeremiah clearly about this and educated him.

At sixteen years of age, "Jeremiah, before I, the Lord, formed, created you in your mother's womb, belly, Jeremiah, I know you! Jeremiah, before you came out of your mother's womb, belly, I did two things: one, I sanctified you, I approved you, and two, I ordained, charged you with holy orders."

My readers, wake up — Jeremiah has taken the same path as Jesus. Jeremiah had to be spiritually fed to be able to identify who really, he is, irrespective of his age, his parents, and recognizes that he was sanctified and he is ordained — not by a pope, a pastor, but by God!

Now Jeremiah is called as a prophet to the nations but had to labor for forty years with the people of Judah — who Jeremiah had problems with, just as Jesus with the Jews.

It is the same way the seed of faith is planted and watered daily by what's plugged in us all to shine globally.

Jeremiah had a speech impediment? Yes, he did, but his faith allows him to bathe his prophecy in tears of compassion.

The weapon Jeremiah had to use? **Faith!** Just as the weapon David had to kill Goliath — not the bow and arrow, but faith!

Jeremiah had to do a mind change. For over forty years, his heart had to change — just as the song requested for the Lord to change our heart.

Let's stop at **2 Corinthians 5:17** —

"For our light affliction, which is but for a moment, worketh for us a far more exceeding and eternal weight of glory... but the things that are not seen are eternal."

(Romans 8:1) —

"There is therefore now no condemnation to them which are in Christ Jesus, who walk not after the flesh, but after the Spirit."

Old things are passed away; they are gone. We cannot see them again!

FAITH — we are challenged and can be challenged by seducing spirits, that is, spirits that *try* leading us in improper behavior, clean and unclean. Let us make a stop at **2 Corinthians 2:11** — *Lest Satan should get (note... the word gets and not take — a big difference — it's a proposed battle; faith vs fear); "us" — this is who? My family? No! It's us, God and me.*

Did it not say the battle is not ours? **2 Chronicles 20:15** — *Be not afraid nor dismayed by reason of this great multitude; for the battle is not ours, but it's God's,* Amen!

An advantage of us: *For we are not ignorant of his devices... and have no rest in my spirit, but thanks to God who causeth us always to triumph (in Christ).*

Deuteronomy 20:4 — *For the Lord, our God, it is He who goes before and with us, to fight against the enemies, and save us and gives us our victory.*

John 5:39 clearly states, words from God Himself — *Search the Scriptures; for in them you have eternal life: and they are they which testify of Me, your God.*

Acts 3:2 — *A certain man lame from his mother's womb was carried, whom they lay daily at the gate of the temple which is called Beautiful, to ask alms of them that entered into the temple. Who sees Peter and John about to go into the temple, asked an alms. And Peter, fastening his eyes upon him with John, said, Look on us; and he did, expecting a gift — but not the gift he expected. Peter said, My brother, I have no money, none, but what I have I will give — and in the name of Jesus, my brother, rise up and walk!!!!*

And just as the woman by the pool who went for water, this man went about preaching God's word. *Immediate manifestation of faith offered and faith activated!*

A very important point here: in the Old Testament and in regards to faith — faith is not 2000 years old, not 4000 years old, but **over 40,000 years old!**

In verse 5 — *Our Lord came down and stood and said to them, "If there be a prophet among you, I the Lord will make Myself known, as like Moses who is faithful, and I speak mouth to mouth, in all Mine house."*

Our Lord reminds us in **Micah 4:4** when He says — *For I brought you out of Egypt, and redeemed you out of the house of servants; and I sent them, Moses, Aaron, and Miriam, before you.*

Fear is the opposite of **Faith**, but it matters *the fear is of what or who* — big difference!

We, at times, leave ourselves with options of the faith that dwells in us by not associating or applying it — *faith.* And that gives room for a visit by the enemy called *fear.*

We always say that "I have fear in me," and that is a **lie**, and a big one! We come out of the presence of the Holy Spirit for that to happen. *Joseph stayed in the Holy Spirit fully.*

Darkness (fear) and **Faith (light)** cannot be in the same body — *never!*

Take off that *narcissistic-garment* and put on the *whole armor of our God* — that is faith.

We are never to leave our *faith-door* open to invite doubt or misbelief. The Lord says we are to *shut the door behind us!*

What does **Hebrews 12:1** say? We are to *lay aside, get rid of every weight (fear)* that can easily beset us — destroy them, every ounce!

As we go, we have to do a lot of "lay-aside-ing" and graduate into the *deposit God hath given us.* Because when the doctor gives us a prescription, we go to fill it, yes? But our Lord God Almighty says we are to *lay aside anything that besets us,* because He knows He, the Lord, hath given us our *faith-prescription from birth* — just like Joseph, just like Jeremiah!

So, as there are many physical sicknesses, so too are the afflictions of us, the righteous — but our Lord covers us all from them.

Isaiah 1:19 soothingly reminds us that our faith will always allow us to *eat the fruit of our life* given to us by our Lord.

The freezing of our faith drives us up to a city called **Rebellion**, and the diagnosis of which is **Witchcraft.**

Not using our faith sends us very deep — and we need more help to come out!

Joseph got out easily; the three Hebrew boys stayed in the fire and were not burned, while Jonah had a *whale-belly experience.*

NOTE:

I am doing all this, but nothing happens — why?
Is God not answering my prayers?
Or is He not even hearing me?

You, Lord — Your ears are not deaf, neither Your hands short — but I am not getting answers?

Lord, I am giving my praises unto You, I am giving my glory, I am giving all honor in divine worship, bowing down unto You because You are God alone — but not just for Yourself, but for me, for us, Your children! Amen!

And I/we give all our worship unto You, Lord!

Lord, you promise… "Nothing good will You withhold from me/us who love and worship You, Lord."

In **Psalm 1:3** You reassure me/us:
"We are the trees planted by the rivers of water, prosperity, and our fruits come in all seasons, and everything we do, I do, will never stop but prosper!!!!"

My doors will always be open to prosperity! Amen! Hallelujah!

But… but Lord, I am seeing utter darkness surrounding me — not just from last month, but from last year.

I am at church every Sunday, every Sabbath.
I pay my tithes, I socialize with members, I am honest — and all that, and more.

Lord, my credit is destroyed.
My bank accounts are closed.
My wife divorced me, and I have lost my house and my home!

Lord, I am totally forsaken by You!

Lord, I trust You totally. I speak in tongues, I prophesy.
Where are You, Lord?

Lord, I read my scriptures daily, pray daily.
When will we order a postmortem?

Let's look at the **conscious and the subconscious** — the part of the mind that processes information and influences behavior without our conscious awareness.
And we are not aware every time, and it will confuse and jerk our faith.

The mind — it will stand, not sit down, in our faith-path!
And closes the doors on me, on us, from our faith-house.

Yes, Lord, I say, "You have granted me/us faith."
You have given me/us trust — and these are things which passeth all understanding — yes, You have, Lord!

I am still screwed into my socket as the bulb; my switch is on — why, why is there no light, Lord?

Now, Lord, I am seeking You while You will be found.

Acts 17:28 — "Lord, in You I live, and in You I move, and in You I have my being."

Lord, I am not hearing from You...
Speak, Lord, thy servant heareth!

BLESSINGS VS THE EFFECTS OF THE BLESSINGS ...

Proverbs 10:22 clearly states, "The BLESSING of our Lord makes us RICH, and HE (Who? The LORD GOD ALMIGHTY) adds no sorrow with it." The original Hebrew literally says, "The Blessing of our LORD, it makes RICH!" So, we are to see clearly what it—the Scripture—says: it is ONLY BLESSINGS we receive, and no sorrow, no discomfort, no pain is attached to it (Blessings)! It comes by itself!

And because of the negative meaning added, it helps to destroy our FAITH! There are certain Scriptures I do not SPEAK; I do not READ. Thank GOD, HE has established a COVENANT with ABRAHAM, our earthly father, in RICHES which is passed on to us, shown in Deuteronomy 18:18: "And YOU shall remember the LORD your God, for it is HE who gives us power to obtain wealth."

A point of interest is that "…for it is HE, our God, who GIVES the power REQUIRED to OBTAIN wealth." Hallelujah! Which brings us back in the circle with—yes, you got it—it is the WORD, FAITH! Note it requires THE POWER to OBTAIN. What power? THE FORMULA in BUILDING, MANUFACTURING, RESURRECTING FAITH.

Psalm 1:3 says what? Our GOD has PLANTED us FIRMLY by the STREAMS, and we WILL YIELD fruits in all SEASONS without any withered leaves and will bear plenty, bountifully!

The point of interest is that this COVENANT was not only made with and to ABRAHAM, but also with Isaac, Abraham's son! And yes, Abraham and Isaac believed God, and it is counted as righteousness (in the Old Testament, Galatians 3:3). Paul reaffirms the same and shows that God always treated FAITH in the same mode—as righteousness!

We must look carefully at how God describes the Galatians in Chapter 3:3 and called them FOOLISH. Let us take a rest at the same Galatians 3, at verse 7, that clearly states: "Know ye therefore that they which are of FAITH, THE SAME ARE THE children of ABRAHAM, and in THEE, Abraham, will ALL NATIONS be blessed!" Hallelujah! For the just, the righteous, will live by FAITH! ACT LIKE YOU KNOW IT, UNTIL YOU BECOME IT!!!

Ephesians 5:1 … WATCH, LOOK, MIMIC what GOD does; John 3:16; Proverbs 20:11; James 2:14—Action, not just TALK!

Empathy of Religion (ability to share and understand the feeling of another; being sensitive to, vicariously experiencing the feelings either of the past or present). There are three types:

1. Cognitive—simply being aware of another person's emotional state.
2. Emotional—engaging with and sharing those emotions.
3. Compassionate—taking action and supporting other people.

Jehovah Rapha (Hebrew), the GOD who HEALS (Exodus 15:26), Provider—Jireh; Jehovah Nissi, in the Bible only once—Moses held the Rod of God (The LORD is Our Banner) Exodus 17:15. As Moses lowered his hands, he lost, but holding his hands UP—VICTORY!!!

Mary gave birth at sixteen, Abraham's fathered at ninety-nine— anything can and will happen in between!—Jesus' disciples said, "This is a deserted place; send them, the 5000 men, away to the villages to buy!" But Jesus said, "Give them something to eat. You have two fishes and five loaves, bring them to me."

My Disciples—without FAITH I am leaving myself outside, like the Prodigal Son, but I am, we are, to mimic Psalm 31:7, and we are to REJOICE in God's LOVE and walk away from the AFFLICTION, walk away from the ANGUISH of our soul.

My friends, show the FACE God hath given—the face of joy, the face of peace—that our God hath showered upon us, who HE hath taken out of a besieged lifestyle and hath preserved us because of being FAITHFUL to HIM.

And stop right here, my brothers, my sisters, as this FAITHFULNESS breeds our labor of love to our FATHER which brings the offspring by the Holy Spirit—and that FAITH! FAITH? No, it is not a thing, it is the SPIRIT OF GOD that is PLANTED in us by Romans 12:3!

If you never know any other Scripture, know these two: God hath given us a measure of faith, and "without FAITH we can never please HIM!"

So, we are all to be happy, be glad, be contented, for we will always be afflicted—in anguish of not just the body, the mind, but—yes, you got it—the SOUL! The woes that cometh from the spirit of darkness, yes, they are there—and they are there to do what? Answer me, what? To bring FEAR!

And what does FEAR do? It makes us anxious, scared, panicked, sleepless, etc., and makes us vulnerable. But FEAR is not from our LORD—not earthly fear! Which is of the devil—that fear Satan tried to incite when HE went to the Cross and died. Satan does come to visit us when we are most vulnerable, and the weapon we have to use there and then is FAITH!

Yes, David killed Goliath with what? (Smile) No, not the stone—with the FAITH David had! Remember that the Scripture says if we have the FAITH the size of a mustard seed (2cm), we can and will REMOVE MOUNTAINS!

And my friends, do not live with the initial size of the seed because it grows into the largest tree—and so will our FAITH.

Peter asked JESUS, "If it is you, Master, bid me come." When the mother feels the labor pain, what does she do? Peter was "feeling his labor pain." Peter wanted to have "conceived faith" and do like the "three Hebrew boys."

Are you "feeling labor pain" now—for your exam results? To be accepted in college? To be married? To get a job? To get a good doctor's report? To go live in your own house or condo? To start dating? To overcome your sexual urges? To get a visa?

Do not let doubt induce fear in us, in me, because the eyes of our LORD are passing over us who FEAR HIM—reverential fear!!! Psalm 33:18—with our HOPE buried in GOD'S unfailing LOVE.

Let's walk through the path we take from birth to adulthood.

Does that baby have any FAITH? No? Maybe? Yes? Of course, that baby has faith!

Does the baby open and shut its eyes? Does the baby cry? Does the baby suck its mother's breasts? Does the baby know Mom? YES! YES! That child TRUSTS what its mind sees, what its eyes see—that TRUST is its FAITH!!!

When GOD spoke with Mary, when GOD spoke with Jeremiah, when GOD spoke with the Hebrew boys, when GOD spoke with Abraham, etc.—what do we see, what do we understand? FAITH is BORN IN US just as oxygen, and it's that FAITH that allows the day-old child to breathe!

Now, was that child breathing before? No, yes, maybe? That child was breathing before birth!!!

Psalm 36:5 (57:10) tells us GOD'S FAITH in us goes very far, very back—FAR—to the heavens, to the skies. How far out have we launched our FAITH? GOD'S love is better than LIFE (Psalm 63:3), so David says, "I will GLORIFY YOU, LORD!"

This FAITH that we build and keep building has so much space we will never "reach" GOD'S APEX!!! For as high as the heavens are above this earth, so is GOD'S LOVE and the FAITH handed unto us—and all we need is to FEAR HIM—reverential fear!

It is HIS COVENANT—HE hath given unto us HIS FAITH—to live in us! We are to be in such a RELATIONSHIP with GOD—Mr. and Mrs. LOVE-FAITH—where they both KISS each other, as in Psalm 85:10.

Such command is given to us in Proverbs 3:3: "Never let LOVE, never let FAITH go away from us, but we are to bind them both around our neck and WRITE them on the tablet of our HEART!"

Ecclesiastes 5:10: "Whosoever loves MONEY never has money; whoever loves wealth is never satisfied with his or her income."

Isaiah 43:4: "Since you are PRECIOUS and honored in my sight, and because I love you, I will give men in exchange for your life."

And in Isaiah 54:10: "Though the mountains be shaken and the hills be removed, my unfailing LOVE for you will not be shaken nor my COVENANT of peace be removed," says the LORD your GOD, "who has compassion on you."

Can I ever seek more re-assurance from my GOD to us? No! Because if I love money, my trust—my faith—will be buried there. So, when money says goodbye, what will I have left? NOTHING!

FAITH is not something that can be taken away from me, and I cannot give it away! What we allow to happen with FAITH is that we do not use it!

Is water in your pipe? Yes? Turn it on!!! FAITH without works is dead!

Let us stop at 2 Corinthians 5:17: "Therefore, if anyone be in CHRIST, they are a new creature; old things are passed away, and all things become new!"

It is very important for us, children of God, to recognize this RE-BIRTH, as this brings us back to be a new person. We are in a new body, and we are to allow the HOLY SPIRIT to really be living in us, and our spiritual ear—not ear—hear when HE speaks!

We need to surrender—not just go to church—but surrender our whole life to HIM! That is TRUST, and that is where our FAITH-BUTTON is turned on!

When we get married, what did we do? Invite our spouse into our heart! That is exactly what GOD does when HE visited us—not last week, but over 2000 years ago!

Psalm 23:6: "Surely goodness and love follow me all the days of my life, and I reside in the house of my FATHER forever."

And Psalm 26:3 says loudly: "Your love is always before us, and I walk daily, continually in it, and I am in your house, your presence, where you live and where all your glory dwells."

I NEED PROOF THAT I HAVE FAITH, SAYS THE MOTHER.

In your hands, what do you have? Your first child! Put her down so she can walk—yes, put her down! As the mother of that child, I take full responsibility for the care and the love of my daughter, my first child!

Let's go across and compare it with your FAITH—you have none!

A few months later, you leave your daughter on the settee and slip away for three minutes, and—wow! —your daughter fell and is crying, crying! And you, giving her all of Mom's love, your daughter stops and wants her bottle!

Inside, that daughter has the ability to "cry" and "tell" Mom, *I am hurt!* But Mom never taught her daughter to cry. How did she know that? It is born in her!!!

It is the same way FAITH is born in all of us! (Romans 12:3; Romans 11:6).

And just as the child becomes of age, so will FAITH subsequently grow and manifest itself in us—when we allow it—to work! FAITH is "water in us," and we only need to give it room to show who we are through the GOD that lives in and through me, through us!

Let us pull over to a stop in 1 Corinthians 2:9:

"Eye hath not seen, nor ear heard, neither have entered into the heart of man the things our GOD hath prepared for us that love HIM."

What I point out here is that GOD'S WORD says *eye* and *ear* in a singular form—and I ask, why? We have two ear and two eyes! But the *ear* and the *eye* are not natural eyes and natural ear, but spiritual.

And just as we have spiritual eye and spiritual ear, so we have—not *will have*, but *have*—FAITH! FAITH that does not need an adjective before the noun!

So, FAITH is *the Word*, like unto GOD, unto JESUS, unto HEALING—not imaginary but real as GOD!

Where are the mountains? Let's go to Matthew 17:20:

"If we have (even) mustard-seed faith, we can speak to the mountain, mountains, and they will hear and walk away!"

We will say to the mountain of sickness, to the mountain of poverty, to the mountain of divorce, "Be moved," and it will move!

It did not move? Why? Look good—what is it you have in your heart? Doubt! And doubt can—and never will—please GOD!

Now I see where our mind went into another lane, going the same direction, because we searched our heart and found no doubt. So why am I not getting my prayers answered?

Good question—but show me your answer. Could it be iniquity that I am harboring? Is it "hidden sins?" They are not hidden—GOD sees them, and you too!

We looked at iniquity before, and we see it again. Why? Remember, the pigs wanted somewhere to hide. Why do we offer space in our body to be a grave, and not the lighthouse to the world?

My friends, you are reading about someone who is walking out of a past full of utter darkness, who is now beholding that city—great city—up on the hills and in full glance of our LORD GOD ALMIGHTY!

Ever dreamt this would be? No! That is what the LAMB does!

John 1:29, where John sees JESUS coming, and said, "Behold the LAMB…" John recognizes HIM.

Who is John? A man. But whom did he recognize? GOD! (If you see me, you see the father).

FAITH is always available as our energizer, because I stopped by Romans 7:24, where Paul the Apostle had to go to the Bank of Faith with his withdrawal slip and said:

"O wretched man that I am! Who will rescue me from this body of death?"

JESUS placed John in a favorite place. Why? Eagerness to learn—plus John's faith—that's what stood out: John's faith!

John the Evangelist—Gospel of John, Revelation, and the Epistles of John—he wrote.

He learns it's *Faith first*, then effort—not the other way around. Start the car first, then put it in gear.

The eagle has wisdom—so do we! The eagle comes to earth and picks up its prey, the snake, and takes it back up to high altitude. The snake has lost its dominion—the earth.

Is this what our LORD did with Satan?

"Wherefore, seeing we also are compassed about with so great a cloud of witnesses, let us lay aside every weight and the sin which doth so easily beset us, and let us run with patience the race that is set before us!"

This cloud before us—who set it? And why? Our answer is right here:

"We are looking unto JESUS, the Author and Finisher of our FAITH, who for the joy that was set before Him endured the cross—despising the shame—and is set down at the right hand of the throne of GOD."

Jacob had twelve (12) sons, with Joseph his favourite, and Jacob sold him to the Egyptians.

Ask yourself, please—have you ever been sold? And to whom? And who sold you?

Please do a search on yourself just now, so you can have a "Faith-bath" for the new "spiritual garments" you have to wear from now on!!!

Taking off the roof was a perfect exhibition of trust, i.e. faith—and it pleased GOD/JESUS.

Acts 16:16–40 shows Paul and Silas' exhibition—wrote the New Testament—in prison.

FAITH VS PRAYER — WHICH ONE COMES FIRST?

Which has first mention in the Bible?

Faith is the only key that opens doors that shut out doubt.

We always do this — look for the object, by error, when we are to be looking **to** the object — **FAITH!**

The Scripture says to:

"Look unto Him, the Author and Finisher of our faith."
Amen!

Let us remember this always —

Without faith it is impossible to please Him.

Let's look at **Job 1:6–12**, with the battle Job was having with Satan. Jesus says to Satan:

"Satan, I will leave Job all by himself (faith), just as I did with David and Goliath! Just as I did with the three Hebrew boys, and so will I leave you for your present-day situations!"

Let's ask ourselves —
Who sleeps the most, my faith or me?

Where is that coming from?
As the Lord asks us,

"Is it I who lives in you?"

He says,

"I have not given (past tense) you, My children, a spirit of fear, but I have willed you all My Spirit of love and a sound mind."
(2 Timothy 1:7)

This is given to us all — so we are lacking nothing, **nothing!**

The Lord solidifies this in **Jeremiah 29:11**:

"For you know the plans I have for you — to prosper..."

So, negative forces do not always come to pull us down,
but will come to pull us up — to build us up,
to send us where we are to go for our full-time ministry.

Let's look at **Abraham**, who had to go where he did not know,
and so did **Joseph!**
And so **Mary**; a teenager, to have a child to be fathered not by her husband!

None of them went to Bible school, nor were they born to an earthly king!

2 Corinthians 4:7 —

"But we (who) have this treasure in earthen vessels (who), that surpassing all by God, through who? Us."

And **2 Timothy 1:11 —**

"For the weapons assigned to us are never carnal, not physical, but mighty through our assigned faith, through God, in the pulling down of so-called strongholds — adultery, fornication, lying, deceitfulness, covetousness, hate."

In **Ephesians 6:11–15**, the command is given that as children of God, we are to "put on the whole armor," not partial —
that identifies who we really are — living in, dwelling in **faith.**

Why do I need it? To please Him.

Why do I need to please Him? So, we will have an undivided relationship.

What are the results?

We will have His peace that surpasses all understanding!

Will it please me?

Oh my, what joy it brings to our soul!

Are there any benefits for me?

A lot! Just imagine when Peter could say,

"Silver and gold have I none, but such as I have, give I unto you!"

We need to show who we really are and fulfill the saying,

"Trouble only lasts for a while."

Faith is our generator on standby.

Do not give up — faith is dwelling in us.

Never lose our identification — **faith.**

It is not really, we that live, but it is **Christ Jesus, our hope of glory!**

We are bigger than problems, bigger than confrontations, bigger than poverty, marital attack, and the tears.

If we are born in the USA, we are? **Americans! Amen!**
And so does all others that are born in the US, yes?

So, if we are firstly born in the Spirit, who are we?
Christians, children of God!

So, the pronouncement of God through faith lives in us, yes?

The Word of God, through the Bible, tells us over thirty times about
faith,
and that is planted in all of us, yes?

Let's take a peep at **2 Corinthians 5:7**:

"For we live by faith, and without faith we are dead!"

Active faith imposes a 1000% trust set so in all of us by Jesus through
the Holy Spirit.

Faith is the **first meal** God gives to us,
as we are to be pleasing in His sight.
Amen!

As He tells us,

"Without faith, we will not and cannot please Him."
Amen!

God has imparted, inspired, breathed-out **faith** in and to us through the Holy Spirit.

Let's take a peep at **Romans 10:17**, which clearly states and reminds us:

"The implanted faith has already come — not will come — through hearing God's Word."

Faith governs the mind, and the eyes are governed by the mind — the reservoir of our faith

1 John 4:4 clearly tells us who we are:

"God's little children, in whom God lives."

Hallelujah!

And Lord, we thank You for Your decree that established unto us to walk in that light that shows us the way preset before us. **Amen! Hallelujah!**

As we walk through "**customs**" and are welcomed by "**family**," many people smiling with us — we recognize that we really were lifted up from this "earth," and people are **coming to us**, as in the **John 12:32 experience. Hallelujah!**

And we feel this change — pleasant and reassuring — as finally we are **strong in You, Lord,** and feel the full power of You might, wearing Your whole armor that allows us to stand in the liberty with which You have set us!

Thank You, Lord!

And as we go to collect our bags…
(……………………………………)
and pay our duty…
(……………………………………)

2. A Living Soul

Is my soul dead? If so — *dead to what?*
Our soul dies when it is **disconnected from faith**, when it loses the breath of God.
Because **faith is the oxygen the soul breathes.**

Without faith, we begin to suffocate under doubt, fear, and self-reliance.
But when we hear His call and come to Him, our soul begins to **live again** — not *may live*, but **will live.**

3. The Everlasting Covenant

God says, *"I will make an everlasting covenant with you — My faithful love promised to David."*

- **Everlasting** means without end — unbreakable, beyond time.
- **Covenant** means a divine agreement sealed by promise and blood — God's Word sworn to our destiny.

The same love God showed to **David**, He now extends to **you** — to every servant who obeys His voice.

He calls not only His *children*, but His *servants*, *assigned by the Holy Spirit*, to live according to His perfect will — just like Adam, Peter, Mary, Jeremiah, and Lazarus.

4. Faith: The Seed, the Switch, the System

Faith is the **mustard seed** planted within every believer.

When we thirst and have nothing — no money, no means, no strength — God says:

"Come, buy, and eat; come, drink without money and without price." (Isaiah 55:1)

Faith is the **currency of Heaven** — not dollars, but divine trust.

It is the **switch** we turn on when all else fails.

Like when every credit card declines, the tank reads empty, and there's no gas station in sight — but then, God fills your tank supernaturally.

That is **faith in action** — the unseen supply of the Everlasting Covenant.

5. Living in the HOF — The House of Faith

We are residents of the **HOF (House of Faith)**, which is also the **HOG (House of God)**.
Here, faith is our **oxygen**, not material wealth.
In this house:

- There is **no room for sickness**, only a room of **perfect health**.
- There is **no room for poverty**, but a room of **divine provision**.
- There is **no room for fear**, but a room of **courage and praise**.

Just as the Ark was Noah's refuge and Eden was Adam's garden, the **House of Faith** is our dwelling place in God.

6. Mountains and Valleys

Faith lives on the **mountain**, not the valley.
God gave us **mountains** — places of revelation, victory, and divine presence.
The valleys hold **dry bones, sickness, and death**, but the mountains echo with **health, riches, and life**.

At Calvary, Jesus went to reclaim the **keys of darkness**, giving us authority over every valley experience.

7. Abide in Me

The Lord says:

"Abide in Me, and I in you."

Faith teaches us to speak to **mountains**, not to fear them.
It reminds us that our **father's covenant** cannot be shaken or removed — even when the mountains crumble or the hills disappear (Isaiah 54:10).

His love remains, His peace endures, His covenant stands forever.

Closing Reflection

Faith is not theory — it's **oxygen**.
It's not stored in our minds but **breathed through our souls**.
Every time we trust, we inhale Heaven.
Every time we doubt, we lose our breath.

So today, **turn on your Faith Switch**, dwell in the **House of Faith**, and live out the **Everlasting Covenant** He has established with you —

just as He did with Adam, Joseph, Mary, and David.

"Without faith, it is impossible to please God."
— Hebrews 11:6

Chapter 3

Rehab, a prostitute living in the pagan city of jericho (**Joshua 2:10**) told the spies she heard how the Lord dried up the water of the Red Sea for him, Joshua, and utterly destroyed the two kings of the Amorites, who were on the other sides.

The Lord Jesus Christ did not refuse to develop communication with her, the prostitute, because **Romans 12:3** says He, God, hath given each man, each woman, their own level of faith — **everyone!**

That is exactly what she used to run back to the city — not as the person who left, but as the person she now is. **Hallelujah!**

What happened here?
A prostitute now gone to minister? Her spirit is renewed; her focus has changed — because **faith was born in her.**

How? **THAT IS TO BRING US INTO A RELATIONSHIP OF CLOSENESS**

And nothing will ever separate us — it is **Agaphy Love!**

It says, "Let the MIND of CHRIST be in ME ALSO," that is in **Philippians 2:5.** But did not that same Christ Jesus say, *"When you see ME, you see the Father? YES YOU SEE THE (MY) Father but also who else? You see me, you see her, hallelujah!"*

GOD says, *"Thy KINGDOM come on EARTH just as it is in HEAVEN,"* and reminds us that **we**, yes, **we**, will do **greater things** than Christ Jesus hath and will do!

And I will keep pointing out — GOD calls HIS SON, **CHRIST JESUS!**
Why? Why not Jesus Christ?

Jesus Christ was the Son who went to the **CROSS** for us, but when He rose, He became **Christ Jesus!**
Christ Jesus is He who now lives in all of us!!!

John 1:32 – *And John bare record, saying, I saw the Spirit descending from Heaven like a dove, and it abode upon Him.*

John 9:3 – *And Jesus answered, Neither hath this man sinned, nor his parents: but that the works of GOD should be made manifest in him (blind from birth, told him to go to the Pool of Siloam and wash).*

John 4:32 – *But He said unto them, His disciples, "I have meat to eat that thou know not of."*

John 4:14 – *Jesus answered and said unto her, "Whoever shall/will/may drink of this water I give to you will never thirst"* — again, here **faith is put in gear, faith is activated** — *it is a well of living water springing up into (our) everlasting life.*

Hebrews 2:6 – *What is man, that thou art mindful of him (man)? Or the Son of Man, that thou visitest him?*

Verse 7 – *Thou madest him a little lower than the angels; thou crownest him with glory and honor, and didst set him over the works of thy hands.*

Let's stop here — we are made a **little lower than the angels**, yes? This is not a **geographical reference**, but a **spiritual status**, **Hallelujah!**

GOD reminds us in the **Lord's Prayer** of our power of **binding and loosing!**
We have such power, by **faith-assignment**, totally!

1 SAMUEL 15:22

1 Samuel 15:22, where Samuel the prophet told King Saul what our God prefers.

Here, **2 Corinthians 1:9** loudly says to us,

"We are not to trust in ourselves, but in God who raises the dead."

Every athlete has to do a lot of training before and during their operative years. It is the same with us and faith —

"Faith without works is dead!"

We see this in **James 2:26** — just as the body without spirit.

Stop right here, my readers — yes, a stoplight — just as the body without breath is dead, so too without faith.

Take a look at your spiritual odometer — how much gas, petrol, is in your tank? You see half a tank? How far will that take you — another 35 miles? But you are 85 miles away from your destination, are you? Yes!!! It is a confrontation, and you are asked to show the *works of faith*.

What are you going to do? I didn't even open my mouth, and what happened? The needle moved — it did — even at 9:55 PM, to about a quarter tank!

Let us understand when He, God the Father, says we are never to lean on our own understanding — that's what He means (2 Corinthians 1:9).

Our body — we are to be fully aware that this body belongs to… you got it right — this body we call ours belongs to our Lord God Almighty. It's His temple, His sanctuary — He resides there!

Hebrews 12:1 —

"Wherefore, seeing we also are compassed about with so great a cloud of witnesses, let us lay aside every weight and the sin which doth so easily beset us, and let us run, not walk, with patience the race that is set before us, looking unto the Lord Jesus Christ, who is the author and finisher of our faith."

Here, we have to really understand what we are being taught — that for a very long time we have not been men with a spirit, but rather **we are a spirit with an earthly body**.

Colossians 2:10 speaks to us — we are to put on the new man, not Adam, but me — which is renewed in knowledge after the image, the likeness of Him (God Almighty) that created me (myself).

Where there is neither Greek nor Jew, American, Jamaican, Haitian, etc. Paul names at least fifteen, bond nor free.

We spend so much time away from who we really are.

Galatians 3:26 reassures us,

"For we are all the children of the Lord God Almighty by the faith (which is) in Christ Jesus. For all of us who have been baptized into Christ have (already) put on Christ."

We are fully attired in faith — from head to toe, from inside out.

Joseph had it, and let me ask, "Where did he get it from?"

We must be reassured like **Psalm 89:27**, which says,

"I will make him (him who?) my firstborn, higher than the kings of the earth, and my mercy will I keep for him for evermore, and my covenant will stand fast with him (who?) and his seed will endure forever."

Revelation 5:3 —

"No man in heaven, nor in earth, neither under the earth, was able to open the book, neither to look (scroll) thereon. And I wept much because no man was worthy."

Why? Our level of faith. But is faith not available? It is — it is born in us!
It is **spiritual oxygen!**

Luke 4:36 —

"And they were amazed, and spoke among themselves, saying, 'What a word is this! For with authority and power He commandeth the unclean spirits, and they come out.'"

Colossians 2:8-9 —

"For though I be absent in person, yet am I with you in the spirit."

Amen! Humility yields honor — such steadfastness through faith.

Proverbs 15:33 —

"The fear of our Lord begins wisdom." Amen!
And the birth of knowledge and manifestation.

Proverbs 16:3 —

"Commit thy thoughts unto the Lord, and thy goals are (easily) accomplished,"
as faith is not just a noun but more so a verb — it must have action!

Proverbs 3:1 —

"My son, keep my commands (not commandments) and do not forget my words in your heart — the sacred place!"

Galatians 3:2–12, **Romans 4:12**, **John 4:12** —
(Commandments vs. Commands)

John 14:15–17 — Grace = an endowment of power.

Matthew 11:28 — Take My yoke = birth, mimic Me (God).

Genesis 4:3 — And Abel brought the first yielding of his flock (vs. Cain brought from the ground — a big difference).

James 4:1–17 — To whom? To him who lives his life in adultery, our Lord offers grace abundantly. *(12/11/22)*

Jeremiah 2:31, **Mark 10:19–28**, **Deuteronomy 8:12–20**, **John 15:1** — Harvest.

Luke 13:7, Mark 11:13, Isaiah 56:1–8 —
You belong here. *Christian (Child of God)* is really *a little Christ.*

Judges 6:13–16 — The Lord sent a direct message via an angel to Gideon and said,

"I, the Lord, am with you, O mighty man of valor!"

Our Lord reminding Gideon: "I, your God, am still with you. Use the faith I give you to defeat this fear that you are allowing to overcome you mentally!"

So, we are reminded to

"Let the mind of Christ be also in us!"

Gideon — go in faith, go in the strength I have given you, and you will be victorious against nations!

Matthew 11:28 tells us our hope empowers love, empowers purpose, and puts in us the main fruit we need to bear — **faith.**

We remember the **fig tree that bore no fruit**?

James 1:17 —

"Every good gift and every perfect gift is from God, who is the Father of lights, with whom there is no variables, no changes, neither any shadow of turning."

1 John 1:5 says,

"This then is the message which we have heard of Him and declare unto you: that God is light, and in Him is no darkness, none at all."

1 Peter 1:7 —

"The trial of our faith, being more precious than gold that perisheth — though it be tried with fire — is found unto praise, honor, and glory at Jesus Christ."

1 Peter 2:9 loudly says,

"But we are a chosen generation, a royal priesthood, a holy nation, a peculiar people, to show forth praises unto Him who hath called us out of darkness into marvelous light, abundant faith, and it shines gloriously!"

1 Peter 4:12 —

"My beloved, my children, do not think it strange concerning the fiery trial which comes as it is to try you, as though some strange thing happens to you."

Verse 13 —

"But rejoice."

IN GENESIS, God recognized Abraham's faith as righteousness, not religious—huge difference! He, God, saw trust, and God justified Abraham as true belief.
(VIP – Church never existed then!)

Do you have it? Or is it not necessary? Where does it come from? **Jesus** is the **Perfector of our Faith**. Faith is our *spiritual GPS*—it guides us on our pathway, and it is the *currency of Heaven* that is blessed to us to use daily, minutely.

What will someone think of us going on a life journey with an empty "tank"? It is deemed foolish! God says that if we do not possess faith, it is impossible to please Him!

What's the difference? Please remember, faith is given to us all (**Romans 12:5**). And for us to procure faith—to earn it, to garner it, to reap it, acquire it, to obtain it, to get hold of it—we must live holy, totally!

The Lord reminds us: if we harbor iniquity in our hearts but yet pray, we will not hear from Him! It is not just scriptural—it is a real-life story we pass through. And note, I said *"we."* That was sold to me even as an elder in church—yes, me!

Darkness never prevails in light; sin never prevails in righteousness—only when we leave, come out of His presence. Do not, for one-tenth of a second, forget our *spiritual responsibility* to exhort His name—always and all ways.

We are made in His image (**Genesis**) and in **Isaiah 48:10**, take a peep: *"See, I have refined you (us)... I have personally taken away the rough edges, taken away the unforgiving spirit, which exposes our lack of loving our 'enemies'—person, place, thing—and that locks out our assigned faith!"*

Are we subjected to tests? Sure! At school, we get tests, yes? We are compared to Job, Abraham, Moses, the Hebrew boys, Daniel, and their tests. And now I, your God, am *exposing you in your personal fire of affliction.*

Remember the other side of the coin: they asked, "What sin did I commit to be going through this?" And God said, "None!" But for us to have full faith, we are to be bold, confident, knowing how we live— pure and holy!

Our faith must always be sober, not drunk. Like Abraham—the only thing he had was God Himself! He, Abraham, had no Bible.

Let your God, my faith buried in you all, rise with you all, as I showed when I came from the grave—victory as to who I am—and like I emulate my Father, so too will you all do!

2 Corinthians 5:7 — *"For we live by faith, and without faith we cannot and will not please... who? God!"*

John 1:5 says loud and clear (KJV): *"And the light shineth in darkness; and the darkness comprehended (overcame) it not."*

Faith is the weight we carry—*spiritual weight*, the *spiritual muscles*—by laying aside and getting rid of the many things that come at us, that we need to throw away because these same things so easily beset us!

How am I going to lose weight? How am I going to be healed? And from what? We are to use what we have planted in us by God when He takes up residence in us!

"I have" (past tense)—the man at the cross with Jesus, Jesus said to him: *"Today you are, not will be, with Me in paradise."* When? Today!!! When will they be in paradise? Right now!!!

When do we turn on our faith button? Tomorrow? No! Right now—it's *now faith!*

The words of this song say: *"My anchor holds and grips, grabs hold of the solid Rock, Lord God Almighty!"*

God's grace opens up for us to get in, and it's in His presence faith is implanted in you and I. Amen!

God sees us as who we are in Him. Jeremiah was seeing himself as a boy, no experience, yes? But how did God see him?

Young men, young women, adults—grab a hold of the faith planted and watered by God and bear the fruits: healing instead of sickness, riches and not poverty!

When God asked Adam, *"Where are you?"* Adam hid himself, yes? Why? Faith planted in Adam told him something was wrong—he knew because faith was already impregnated in him, Adam.

Adam kept asking himself, "What have I lost?" Faith gives a comfort that comes from and through God!

When Jesus asked for the cup to pass from Him, who expected Him to question His Father's assignment? Faith is challenged by God no matter who you are.

And your test at sixteen changes when you become twenty-nine, forty-seven, seventy-eight, ninety-two!

Faith is a *spiritual ladder* we all have to climb—from a babe in a crib, to the Cross, then back to Heaven. Wow!

Look at this and point it back to us, and so will my path be. We go to the gym and lift weights, yes? Why? So too is our spiritual life.

Our faith-weight starts at 10 pounds, then up to 500 pounds, 1000 pounds! Joseph, David, Peter—all went to their own gym. You are at yours now! Look how many pounds/kilograms you are starting off with!

Remember faith—it is the substance hoped for. Prove Him, God, in me, and lift!!!

That marriage in a path of darkness… that promotion at work you are waiting on from last year… or that husband in jail for seven years.

HERE PLEASE NOTE WHO JOB IS…
He is a perfect man, just like Jesus, and yes, Job is upright!

Questions:
(v.15) Was Job's servants slain? They were — all except one.

Here Job did not look at the dead servants (fear), but he used what he still had, and that was what? **Faith!!!**

He saw that he had one servant left — had one still (**Faith**)!

Job lost his sheep — all burned up — lost his camels, killed, except one. And if that is not all, the wind and the storm came (v.19).

This attack will come when I have the time — it comes when I am doing something (else)!!!

Faith and how it shows up unexpectedly — let's look at where we expose ourselves, the area we hide away from, from the pastors to the pulpits… **Tithes and Offering!!!**

OK, do not close the book!!!

I remember I gave my 10%, amen! $50!!!

And a visiting lady pastor, who does not know me, and I was casually dressed, said, *"The Lord says I am to give $1000!"*

That's my income for two weeks!!!

Anyway, I did, but called the church to hold it until... God knows when.

One mind said, *"Check your bank."* Yes!!! It was paid — Monday at 6 AM!!!

So, I said to myself, *You are going to get a big huge check!* And I didn't!!!

But I am taught — God is always teaching me to obey His command — to be obedient, not the $$$$, as obedience is better than the proposed "sacrifice" I think I made!!!

We have to understand why faith pleases God.

Joseph went from **pit to palace**; Paul wrote the Scriptures — yes? Where?
The three Hebrew boys, in the fire — what put them in there? **Their faith!**

That new automobile I bought — you keep looking at, why?

When I drove home the car I just bought, I felt embarrassed because it was not new! I took it back Monday morning, told them, *"It's not new!!!"*

It is very important to look from the side you "cannot" see.

When Jesus said to Peter, *"Go back same place, but a bit further out, go deeper!"* — but did Peter not go there before? **Yes!**

But Jesus gave one change to Peter: *"Throw your net not on the left side, as you usually do, but throw on the right."*

Here Peter wanted to use his personal experience to challenge what God had given him long before he, Peter, was born — and that is **Faith!**

Here Peter was getting a lesson of what God had planted in him and how to use it, as Peter was in a "dead state," where faith without works is dead.

Let's look at **Proverbs 3:5–6**, it says we are never to lean on our own understanding; it will expose us to misunderstanding, but the gifts of the Spirit — **Faith!**

We see the gifts of the Spirit — all nine of them (word of knowledge, increased faith, gifts of healing, gift of miracles, prophecy, the discernment of spirits, kinds of tongues, and interpretation of tongues) — gives our life, as a child of God, a grand total of? **Faith!**

Faith is the key that opens all nine gifts of the Spirit to us and exposes its full manifestation.

We have so many questions on faith — "Oh, it is not something I think about?"

Is it relevant to you being a child of God?

Is it something I get going to church?

Or my pastor will give it to me?

I am saved thirty-seven years; I have been saved six months and have riches — do I need it?

I am born with a disease, a sickness — do I need faith?

I am born in riches — do I need it?

(Proverbs 3:5–6)
Trust in ME, the LORD, with all our heart and lean not on our own understanding; and in all our ways submit to ME, and I will make our paths straight.

(Hebrews 11:1)
NOW faith is the substance (assurance) of things hoped for; the evidence (conviction) of things not seen.

(Hebrews 11:6)
And without faith it is impossible to please GOD, for whoever would draw near to GOD must believe that GOD exists and that GOD rewards those who (us) seek HIM, GOD.

(Hebrews 11:11)
Through faith also Sara herself received strength to conceive seed and was delivered of a child when she was past age because she judged HIM, GOD, faithfully who had promised.

(Ephesians 3:16)
To be strengthened (to resist doubt, be empowered) with might by HIS Spirit (to infuse) in the inner man (us).

(2 Corinthians 5:7)
For we walk, live by faith, not by sight.

(John 3:16)
For GOD so loved the world that HE gave HIS one and only Son, that whosoever believes (faith) in GOD will never perish but has the gift of eternal life.

(John 6:29)
JESUS answered, "The work of GOD is this: to believe in the One HE (GOD) has sent (JESUS, the MESSIAH)."

(John 6:35)
And JESUS said unto us, "I am the Bread of Life; and we that come

to HIM will never be hungry, and we who believe on HIM will never thirst (for or after anything)."

(John 7:38)
He that believeth on ME, GOD, as the Scripture hath said, "Out of his belly shall flow rivers of living waters."

(John 11:40)
And JESUS said unto her, "Said I not unto thee, that if thou would believe, we will see the glory of (our) GOD?"

(John 11:25–26)
JESUS told us, "I am the Resurrection and the Life; and whosoever believes in ME, even when he dies, will live."

(John 20:29)
JESUS said unto Thomas, "Because thou hast seen ME, thou hast believed; but blessed are us that have not seen HIM, our FATHER, but yet we do believe."

(James 1:3)
Knowing this, that the trying of our faith worketh patience.

(James 5:14)
Is anyone among you sick? Let us call on the elders (of the church) to pray over us and anoint us with oil in the name of our LORD.

(James 1:6)
But let us ask in faith, nothing doubting, for he that doubt is like a wave of the sea driven by the wind and tossed.

(Philippians 4:6–7)
Be careful for nothing; but in everything by prayer and supplication with thanksgiving let our requests be known unto GOD... and GOD's peace, that passed all understanding, keeps our hearts and our minds stayed on HIM, JESUS.

(1 Peter 1:8–9)
Whom having not seen, HIS love; with joy unspeakable and full of glory... though now ye see HIM not, yet believing, ye rejoice in whom.

(Mark 9:23)
JESUS said, "If thou canst believe, all things are possible to us that believe."

(Mark 10:52)
And JESUS said unto us, "Go our way; thy faith hath made us whole."

(Mark 11:24)
Therefore, I say unto you, what things soever we desire, when we ask, we pray, believe that we receive them, and we shall have them.

(Romans 1:17)

For in it the righteousness of our GOD is revealed from faith to faith, as written, "The righteous shall live by faith."

(Romans 5:1–2)

Therefore, being justified by faith, we have peace with GOD through our LORD JESUS CHRIST… by whom we have access by faith into HIS grace and rejoice in HIS glory.

(Romans 10:11)

For the Scripture saith, "Whosoever believeth on HIM shall not be ashamed."

(Romans 14:1)

Him that is weak in the faith receive ye, but not to doubtful disputations.

(Matthew 17:20)

And because of our unbelief: for verily I say unto you, if we have a grain of mustard faith, we shall say unto this mountain, "Remove," and it shall so do… and nothing will be impossible.

(Matthew 21:22)

JESUS answered and said, "Verily I say unto you, if you have faith and doubt not, you shall not only do this which is done to the fig tree, but also if we shall say to the mountain, 'Be thou removed and be cast into the sea,' it will be done."

(Luke 8:50)

But when JESUS heard it, HE answered him, saying, "Fear not; believe only, and we are made whole."

(1 John 5:5)

Who is he that overcome the world, but he that believeth that JESUS is the Son of GOD?

(Galatians 3:26–27)

For in CHRIST JESUS we are all children of GOD through faith. As many of us as are baptized into CHRIST are no longer slave or free, for we are one in CHRIST JESUS.

When God says, *"Do not lean on your own understanding,"* He is not calling us weak — He is calling us to **stand strong** in the faith He has already placed within us.

The old hymn says it best:

"On Christ, the solid Rock I stand — all other ground is sinking sand."

Faith is not a wall to lean on; it is the **foundation** upon which we stand. Without faith, we cannot please God. Without faith, we cannot enter His inner court. Without faith, we remain outside, left to our own strength — and that is never enough.

Think of Adam. God placed him in a vast garden — no fences, no boundaries. Did God give Adam faith? Absolutely. Did Adam use it?

Yes, he did! How else could he name all the animals and fish without any prior instruction?

That's faith in action — divine intelligence flowing through human obedience. God said, *"Let this mind be in you which was also in Christ Jesus"* (Philippians 2:5). That same mind — that same creative boldness — was imparted to Adam, to Moses, to David, to Joseph, and in the New Testament, to Peter, to Mary, to the woman at the well, and the man at the pool.

Faith isn't earned through Bible school or study sessions alone — it's **a gift**. Romans 12:3 says, *"God has dealt to each one a measure of faith."*
When I first heard that, I could hardly believe it! I had spent twenty years searching for faith, praying for faith — not realizing it was already within me.

Looking back, I can now see how I used that faith unknowingly.
When I invested $1,800, it turned into $18 million.
When I sowed $30,000, the return came back as $980,000.
Was that my doing? No. It was **God's principle of faith** at work.

Psalm 105:37 reminds us:

"He brought them forth also with silver and gold, and there was not one feeble person among their tribes."

They were protected. Their enemies trembled. While Egypt was seized by fear, God's people were clothed in faith — mustard-seed faith that moved mountains!

That same faith brought the cloud by day to shield them from the sun and the pillar of fire by night to guide them through darkness.
Bread fell from heaven — fully toasted by the fire of God's faithfulness!

Faith is total reassurance — divine trust that never fails.
The coming of Jesus on earth was a **reaffirmation** of that trust. His very presence reassured us of the faith God had already instilled within humanity — purchased at the cost of His Son's life.

Through Scripture, I discovered a foundation to **build a Faith Activator**:

- Twenty **comforting scriptures**,
- Thirty-six **verses of reassurance**,
- Thirty **verses of protection** —
  all spiritual materials to strengthen and activate our faith.

Without faith, we cannot please God.
Without faith, it's like having no driver's license — we cannot move forward.

Faith and worry may live in the same house, but they are never roommates.

In Matthew 6:25, Jesus tells us not to be anxious — not to worry about tomorrow, but to walk boldly and confidently in faith.

In Matthew 11:28, He calls out again: *"Come unto Me, all ye that labor and are heavy laden, and I will give you rest."*

And He still whispers today:

"Call unto Me — you will never get a busy signal.
My peace I leave with you; My peace I give unto you.
Let not your heart be troubled, neither let it be afraid.
For I am in you, and you are in Me."

When you feel weary, cast your burden upon the Lord.
Let Him sustain you; let Him carry you in the hollow of His hand.

Look behind you — what do you see?
One set of footprints.
Not because He left you, but because He was carrying you.

David knew this truth well. In Psalm 86, he prayed:

"Bow down Thine ear, O Lord, hear me; for I am poor and needy. Preserve my soul, for I am holy: O Thou my God, save Thy servant that trusteth in Thee. Be merciful unto me, O Lord, for I cry unto Thee daily."

Can you feel the **earnestness** in David's plea?
That depth of prayer reflects the **level of faith** within him.

Our own faith-o-meter rises with the sincerity of our heart's cry — and yes, God reads it.

From the woman pressing through the crowd just to touch His garment,
to the man by the pool waiting for healing,
to Joseph in the pit — faith was their anchor.

The level of our faith determines the reach of our miracles.
Even when death was declared over a man's life, his faith turned it around.
Faith gives voice to the impossible and strength to the weary.

So, we echo David once more:

"Teach me Thy way, O Lord; I will walk in Thy truth.
Unite my heart to fear Thy name." (Psalm 86:11)

CHANGING OUR PERSPECTIVE

(A point of view, attitude)

VALLEY OF AFFLICTIONS *(Something that causes pain or suffering)*

E.g. We are in the sea and the rain is/about to fall — and what will I do?

Pressure – do we put it in our tires? What about when we are pumped up? What do we do — faith or fear?

Where is the fear coming from? Not from God! How did it get to you?

Pressure (trials) — does it burst pipes, or does it inflate them? What "balloon" is your faith blowing? What size tire are we inflating?

Our faith tires cannot burst, but they can be under-inflated by us — not by God — because He hath given us our own size: 13", 24", 48". *(He hath given each one of us our own measure of faith — Romans 12:3)*

God's faith powered in us is bottomless. God said to Jabez, *"As far as you can see, Jabez, not on My limit, but yours."* The limits are self-imposed.

I went to the car dealer, and he found favor in me and gave me a car, yes, he did. Jabez imposed none on himself and called on God —
1 Chronicles 4:10, *"Oh that Thou wouldest bless me indeed, and enlarge my border, my coast, and keep me from evil."*
And God granted Jabez that which he requested. Amen!

The mistake is, I took it — it was not a new car. So I kept it for three days and took it back, told him I am returning it, and I did — and got? My new car!

And I did that a second time and gave him until 3 p.m. to come get the CRV I chose, and I would not give a deposit. He called me to beg me to come back at 4 p.m. instead. Did I give him my SS number? No!

We look at our credit report just as the mortgage company does, as the car dealer does. Have we ever asked ourselves — am I the same as them? Can I say no? I cannot. Why? Am I really separated?

I went to my bank manager, and he said, "Paul, I am busy, but go to Mr. Cash and tell him to give you what you want."
I wanted $50,000!

When He says, *"Before you open your mouth, I will bless you,"* God says, *"Prove Me now."*

We will go through our "fire," but will it burn us? Gold — very precious, very expensive — but it has to go in strong fire, yes?

Water can appear in three forms — ice, steam, and boiling — is it still water? Am I still human when I am saved? Am I still liking my Father, God?

My reader, stay right here with me and answer this question, please.

Jesus knew John, but how did Jesus know him? John did not know himself, so he disqualified himself to baptize Jesus.

And what is faith? It's the things we hope for, amen, but significantly, we will not see — not with our eyes, but with the Holy Spirit in us!

Remember Jesus said to Peter, about the church on the rock, *"It is not you, Peter, who said that, but it is the Holy Spirit."*

Who better to confirm evidence in us than the Holy Spirit!

It is very wonderful to be able to say, as Peter at Gate Beautiful said — what he does not have (silver and gold) — but such as I have, faith! And use that to pray for manifested healing!

(Hebrews 12:1)

"Wherefore seeing we also are compassed about with so great a cloud of witnesses, let us lay aside every weight, and the sin which doth so easily beset us, and let us run with patience the race that is set before us,
Looking unto Jesus, the author and finisher of our faith… who is set down at the throne of God."

(Psalm 86:12)

"I will praise Thee, O Lord my God, with all my heart: and I will glorify Your name forevermore. For great is Thy mercy toward me, and You have delivered (past tense) my soul (not body) from the lowest hell."

(Verse 6 says)

"Give ear unto my prayer; give ear to my supplications, also."

The **evidence of faith** takes us to **Genesis**, yes!

Yes — David, who committed adultery (with Bathsheba), yes? And murder — yet he is described as **a man after God's own heart**, through **repentance!**

Anyone being in Christ becomes a **new creature** — *when?* B.C. or A.D.?

Is it **what you do**, or is it **who you are**?

Who elevates you?

1 Corinthians 15:9 — "I am the least of the apostles; I persecuted the Church of God."

We should never let ourselves be prisoners of our past.

Philippians 3:12 — "I keep working for which you are called," appended to that *purpose.*

God's **plan and purpose** last forever.

Grace (*2 Corinthians 12:9*) — *Purpose:* to do His will; God's ability; His grace is sufficient.

2 Corinthians 12:7 — Even though... so, to keep me from being proud, conceited.

Philippians 4:13 — **Faith** (*2 Corinthians 12:10*) ... "I can do all things through Christ."

John 4:35 — "Lift your eyes..."

Genesis 11 ...

2 Corinthians 12:14 — Paul says, "I am ready to visit you a third time, because I want you..."

See also **2 Corinthians 12** — *Paul's vision of Paradise.*

Prayer — a plea: *2 Corinthians 12:8*

1 Chronicles 4:9–10 — Jabez

Jabez, like Jacob in *Genesis*, was more honourable than his brothers, but his mother named him **Ja'bez**, meaning he was born in sorrow — not the "gift" a son would want his mother to give.

But your **natural birthplace or circumstances** will never be your **spiritual GPS to your destiny!**

Here, Jabez applied his feet to the **spiritual accelerator** and called out to God:

"Oh, that Thou wouldest bless me indeed and enlarge my border, my coast, and that Thou wouldest keep me from evil, that it (evil, sin) will not grieve me."

Now look at this — Jabez got God's attention, and God said,

"I heard you and have granted you all your request."

Jabez gave a perfect picture of **faith** that's in him. Jonah had to have **faith in deep waters physically**, just as Jabez did **on dry land**.

JOSEPH WAS FIRST PLACED IN THE PIT BEFORE HE GOT IN THE PALACE.

WHERE WAS MOSES BORN? AND WHERE WAS HE RAISED? AND WHERE HE REIGNED?

LUKE 8:40 — (Inject, decree, declare — all three declare FAITH) "...AND IT CAME TO PASS, THAT, WHEN JESUS WAS RETURNED, THE PEOPLE GLADLY RECEIVED HIM: FOR THEY WERE ALL WAITING FOR HIM."

(JAIRUS, A MAN, RULER OF THE SYNAGOGUE, WHO FELL DOWN AT JESUS' FEET ASKING JESUS TO COME TO HIS HOUSE) — FAITH!

Did he know who Jesus is? What is the state of his house? His 12-year-old daughter (with Sahar's daughter) was also there, laying dead.

But before Jesus reached there, comes the woman with the issue of blood for 12 years — a lot of hospital visits, but no healing. She, who had no name, touched the border, the hem of Jesus' garment, and immediately her issue of blood stopped.

And of course, Jesus asked, "Who touched me?"

Peter said, "There is a lot of us here, so it was anyone of us, Jesus." But Jesus knew otherwise — virtue had left Him!

Verse 48:
And Jesus said unto her, "Daughter, be of good comfort: thy faith hath made thee whole; go in peace."

Why did Jesus say to her, "Go in peace"? Is there a relation between the 12 years? Age is 12 and issue of blood 12 years?

Let us look in **LUKE 8:8**, that speaks about the sowing of seeds — that is seed-faith, mustard-seed faith. It is planted in us as faith, and it bears fruits — a by-product of faith.

That one seed planted brings forth what? You got it — more seeds of its own kind — and takes us into a huge plantation of faith.

We have to seek a renewed mind, not the one I perceive, but the one God Himself planted in Adam and is passed on to all of us. That mustard-seed faith becomes 1,000 times bigger, 10,000 times bigger!

Are you sure, Pastor? Remember the fig tree that didn't bear? Was it bearing season? No! But was that an excuse? No!

Are we afraid to challenge what God says? Most of us do. But who was it God told, "You are gonna die soon"? Did he accept that what God said to him? Initially yes, but he subsequently challenged God, and? Got fifteen years' extension!

The faith in us cannot be a candle that beams light but we cover it — no way! We are to see ourselves as God's candlestick of faith. We are to show evidence of the Word in our life.

Remember, God launched the ship with His disciples to get to the other side — and He fell asleep. Why? God knows He hath planted faith in His disciples, because He asked them (**LUKE 8:25**) — "Where is your faith?"

Stop here a second, my friends. God used the word "YOUR FAITH!!!" — not God's faith, not Jesus' faith, but **your faith!**

That's our spiritual identification — just as the cop stops us and the first thing, he/she asks for? An identification. Remember, faith without works, without ID, is dead! Without faith, I cannot please God!

WOW! No faith, no God. Know faith, know God! It's an option.

Every time we use our faith — yes, every time we do — virtue comes out of God, out of Jesus. Even though Jesus was in the crowd, He felt the virtue leaving Him.

How did the woman — not a disciple — want to touch the end of His garment? Say it again — she had faith! And God, Jesus, sent her off in peace.

I ask you — when FPL (the light company) power comes in your house, is it mine or theirs? It's mine. And can I use it? Sure!

What is the difference when we are plugged in to the Holy Spirit? We are afraid to turn on our faith-switch!

Faith is the current from the power of our God that is placed in us all, and we are the bulb to shine to the world — into dark places never before able to be seen. Not just to lead us, but those around us who need that light from God that beams through us!

Jesus consoled them, "Fear not." (**JOHN 11:11**)

Jesus told His disciples that Lazarus was dead — for four days, one day too much (this is to help His disciples know who Jesus is). Jesus requested them not to weep — a faith-building mood.

"Lazarus is only sleeping."

And He took only Peter, James, John, and the parents (**LUKE 8:51**) … and she rose immediately and commanded them to give her meat — food!

Yes, she ate — but let's go across to **JOHN 6:51**, where Jesus said, "I am the living bread that comes down from heaven." Hallelujah!

This is for our main-course meal. Our ancestors wandered hungry in the wilderness, and God provided quail and bread (**EXODUS 16**).

This food gave temporary satisfaction (woman at the well to catch water), but Jesus says, "Whosoever eats His bread — the bread of life — lives forever."

(We are to believe, apply faith, apply trust.)

This is for all spiritual carvings. We have to use it — His blood, His body — as food and drink for our new, unending life, i.e., **FAITH.**

Isaac got instructions, "Do not go to Egypt; stay right here and sow your seeds."

Isaac had to do two sowings — one, his **faith**, and the other, his **seeds.** Please note here, Isaac reaped in the same year he planted and reaped one hundred times what he planted!

Let me ask my readers — did the Lord recognize faith in Isaac? Yes, our Lord sure did! That is why He told Isaac not to leave.

And what is the instruction(s) our Lord has given us? This is to see where our faith level is, and readers, do not worry — we will soon see your **faith-gauge** going up, up! Amen!

What is shown to us are all new. Sorrow is gone, and joy — abundant joy, contentment — is right here with and in me! Look at the help: **God the Father, God the Son, and God the Holy Spirit — all three!** That is the magnitude of my faith.

We each got our own measure. This faith I give to you is all yours! As I, God, asked Moses, "What is it you have in your hands?" so say I, God, unto you — what level of faith do you have? I gave it to you just as I gave Jeremiah at sixteen years of age!

Use it! It is a command — use it!

Look at the pair of shoes you have on — when was it made? Five (5) years ago. But when did you buy it? Last month! It is the same with faith — it was "made" with Me 40,000 years ago, but I gave it to you when you were born thirty-five years ago. **Use it!**

Mary's womb did not conceive until the Holy Spirit visited her — so it is with you, My son, My daughter. Hallelujah, use it, put it in gear, and drive on!

I am **Alpha and Omega** (Beginning and the End). That is **faith in totality!**

Who said that? None other than our God! Did He not challenge us to "Prove Me"? It is a challenge to us in **Malachi 3.** It is a huge challenge because God asks us for ten percent (10%), but says, "My reward will outgive yours — that you will not have room, have no space!"

Darkness will challenge us — and that's both normal and natural.

Faith is our gift from God at birth, and most times the one who knows it before us? The **spirit of darkness!** And it uses insidious spirits to get at us!

But please remember — the cops will never be looking for you in jail; you are locked up! But the minute, the second you are absent, you are wanted.

This is what happens when we get saved and put on our spiritual attire, our spiritual garments.

The man by the pool was there for many years and began to "live" there. Faith, through Jesus, came to him to offer healing from his sickness, but he found all "excuses." His faith was buried — just like some of us, we cannot find it.

Jesus gave him a **faith-energizer charge**, and what happened?

It is very important to see when sickness or any other faith-test comes to visit us — they come with company. Like that sickness, it brings confinement — spiritual confinement, emotional confinement, financial confinement, parental confinement, mental confinement, physical confinement — and that's just six (6).

In **Acts 14:8** we find this man who is crippled in his feet before he was born, and never walked. He heard the Apostle Paul speak and perceived he had faith to be healed. And what did he, the crippled man, do? He leaped up to those feet!

There is this battle we are to be aware of — we must be aware of — not between flesh and flesh, but between flesh and Spirit, and it will not stop until our Lord God Almighty comes.

Let us see who we are — the tree planted by the rivers, well-watered — but if we are ever rooted up and out, we sure will not grow, but wither and die.

We must use the **Spirit regulator**, not the **mind regulator.**

God planted seed-faith in all of us, and we are now serving God — five, eleven, twenty-eight years — and we see no fruit, none?

Pray, study your Word, reason with Him, the Lord God, and He will show you the path.

He says, "Those who hunger and thirst after righteousness (**Matthew 5:6**) will be filled!" Hallelujah!

Ephesians 3:20 clearly says,

"Now unto Him that is able to do exceedingly, abundantly above all that we ask or think, according to the power that worketh in us… one Lord, one faith, one baptism."

Our Lord shows the pronouncement of faith placed in us in Ephesians. Look at **verse 11 in chapter 4**, which says,

"…He gave some apostles, some prophets, some evangelists, and some pastors and teachers; for the perfecting of the saints, for the work of the ministry, for the edifying of the body of Christ."

(**Colossians 1:27** — Paul, this is a very expandable scripture, it says a lot, use it — this is personal instructions; still in chapter three)
"To whom God would make known what is the riches of the glory of this mystery among the Gentiles, which is Christ in you, the hope of glory, and teaches every man in all wisdom, and presents every man perfect in Christ Jesus, Amen! Hallelujah!"

We must not trust in **me**, but we are to trust **Him.**

We are to understand both fears — one is **reverential**, and the other is **demonic fear.**

"As often as you do this, you do it in remembrance of Me." Who? God or the devil?

Phobia — afraid of someone or something that cannot harm you/us.

Perceptions cause fear — see the puppy that looks like a dog; see an animal that looks like a lion but is a dog. (Subconscious.)

Romans 16:25 —
"Now to Him that is of power to establish you according to my gospel (whose?), and the preaching of Jesus Christ, according to the revelation of the mystery which was kept secret since the world began, but now is made manifest for the obedience of faith."

Our God gets us well prepared — the cloud by day and our fire by night.

Forget — disremember — is information we already have; it is completely different from ignorance.

Deuteronomy 8:7 —
"For the Lord our God has brought us into a good land with brooks of water (prosperity), fountains and depths that spring out of the valleys and hills (plural, more than one); a land of wheat, barley, vines, fig trees, land of oil, olive, and honey."

Let's pass by **Luke 6:38**, which loudly says,
"Give, and it will be given to us; good measure, pressed down, shaken together and running over into our laps. For with the measure we use, it will be measured back to us."

It is very important to note here — we must give without limitations, because we are being blessed by our Father one hundred times greater!

And we are not in a competition — no!

Our Lord God trusted us in that He who had no sin or sins did what? Died for us. Yes, our Lord has faith in us — **unlimited faith** — so even when we were yet sinners, He went to the cross for us.

And we ask, "What manner of man is this who gave His personal for us?" It is **Jesus** — became who we are, human, so we, human, become who He, Jesus, is!

That is **abundant faith, unlimited faith!**

And please remember that faith — the spirit of darkness knows and recognizes it — when he said to Jesus, "If Thou be the Son of God..." and in **Acts 19**, he said, "Jesus I know, Peter I know..."

We need to know who we are and give proof that we know who we are — that is, have the **active faith**, the **faith in action!**

I heard **1 Samuel 15:22** saying just now,
"Obedience is always better than religious sacrifice."

Our faith must always be used — always! Not taken away by "fat-of-rams" burnt offerings or sacrifices.

But do not misunderstand and ignore **Mark 16:18**,
"That we are to lay hands on the sick, and they will recover."

Here again, faith identifies itself and action takes place — as faith without works, without action, is totally dead.

And when we do not have faith — **active faith** — we cannot please God!

Once we take our feet off the accelerator, our vehicle stops, yes? So it is without applying our faith.

LET'S LOOK OVER IN PROVERBS 1:7

(......) It speaks of **fear**, reverential, of the Lord — this brings us knowledge. So, we now know the Lord just as Solomon says, *"We will, not shall, find all (not some) precious substance, and our houses filled with spoils."*

And to ascend even higher in faith? Slip over to verse 23 — *says You, O Lord, that You will pour out Your Spirit, not pastor's spirit, upon us, me, them, by making Your words known unto us — educate us, prosper us, protect us, guide us, spiritualize us, and fill us!*

The seeds of reverential fear! We are to hearken, listen, hear unto You, our God, and shall be quiet from fear, doubt, afraid of evil, which cometh not of or from God! We are to incline our ear unto Him, unto wisdom, by applying our hearts, our ways to understanding!

Yes, we have to understand (*stand under*) His holy words and live in the Spirit. Remember Romans 12 — the faith God hath given us? How much more reassurance do we need?

Here's some more — *Let not mercy, let not truth forsake me, us, but ask for our Lord to bind our enemy around their necks and write them on the tables of our heart, for the whole world to see me, us, and the fullness thereof; and that the wicked, the enemy, will come, obey in God's holy presence, of which we are part of, Amen!*

Let us enjoy the benefits, the spoils of the faith buried, planted in me, us, and the favor of spiritual understanding in the presence of our Lord — just as David did, just as Abraham did!

Remember Jesus sent Peter back — where? Where he went before. Peter did not have the awareness of the faith already in him, but somehow we — yes, we, me, us — have to develop, grow, what God hath planted in all of us. Do so with all our heart (*Proverbs 3:5*) — do not lean to my understanding, but to Yours, Lord God Almighty!

It is the reward, prize You promise us — where we are joined to You by our navel umbilical cord, both in the Spirit and the marrow to our bones. *Hallelujah!*

I do not want us to "lock ourselves in" to a self-imposed exile and pose a fifteen (15) year sentence — especially when the judge? Yes — is You! Or is your pastor? Your spouse? Your child?

The Lord, our Lord, only needs the honor due to Him. Do not be the Cain who gave "anything"; give the first fruit of his increase! Abel gave the first fruit of his increase — that is Abel's substance.

Without faith? Impossible — can never please God. Remember the widow's mite? It was a few pennies, but what was exposed? Her faith, not the money. God then, through grace, gave her favor — just like in Proverbs 3 — *length of days was given in her right hand and riches and honor in the other hand!*

We must allow the faith to build trust in our God, and that trust is based upon truth — and it is that truth that sets me, you, us free!

Take a look at yourself in the physical mirror — keep looking. Who do you see? Keep looking! Do not stop — look, look until you see the Lord God Almighty! He will show Himself plain before your own eyes!!!!

The Lord is asking, *How long do you want to "date" Me?* We are "engaged" — five months, five years, fifteen years — let us get "married," so I can put on your "faith ring." That is the only time you can please Me.

Hebrews 11:6 — *Without faith it is impossible to please God!*

Be steadfast, unmovable, abiding in His word — just as we trust the prescription our doctor gives.

So, the young man, the young lady thinking of keeping good health — so what they think? You got it! Let's find a gym, and one that we can afford. Because we have to exercise daily and watch out for the results. Am I correct? Yes?

So, we keep going to the gym — two months, three months — and looking out for results. But if we are going to the gym now for seven months, fifteen months, and have paid a lot of money, $3,500 — the gym instructor says, "Paul, you are looking great!" even though I have not lost ten ounces!!! I am not seeing no changes — none!

ATROCITIES — OUT OF OUR RECREATED SPIRIT — LAUNCH OUR WORSHIP (HEBREWS 11)

Let all of You make all of me! Amen.

I looked at **Hebrews 11:1–6**, which vividly says... *Now faith,* not yesterday's — just as Mary had to subsequently (look inside of her today), not tomorrow — yes, today, right now — *is the substance of things I am, had hoped for so, the past six months, six years, six decades,* but yet I see no evidence.

Because we keep looking out rather than looking in unto the Spirit living in me.

Jabez had to look inside of him before he saw the results — a vast stretch of land. So too, Mary, who had no sexual communication, but was pregnant. It is God's grace that umbrellas over us, that privileges us with His gift of faith. It is a seed planted in us!

And if we do not have our spiritual ID — faith — it is impossible to please God!

Faith is not *a* seed, but it is *the* seed planted in Mary, sixteen years of age. Mary did not see the qualification, the honor endowed upon her by God, not her husband.

The birth of confusion enclosed her for sure, but Mary was firstly impregnated with — yes — **faith**, and that allows her to be the mother God chose for His Son's birth!!!

Faith is not a gender, as Peter had to and wanted to experience faith — and did what? Yes, walked on the water.

Faith is the weapon we use to find the needle in our hay-sack!

We should never doubt what our Lord has put into us, what He has given to us, when loudly David said in **Psalm 34:19** — *Many are the afflictions of us, the righteous, but our Lord delivereth us out of them all!!!*

Note the verb *delivereth* — it is past tense. **Hallelujah! It is done already!**

Why do we "look back???"

**"Let Us sit in this STORY of a young Minister on the road, on the side of a Cliff, and was attacked by pounding Rain and flashes of Lightning. WoW, out of the blue, he found Shelter! Hallelujah! And there he wrote? Yes, you got it—ROCK OF AGES... It is a Cleft for Me, let me hide myself in Thee. This young Minister had such BOLD-FAITH; he didn't turn back but PRESS-ON. He could have thought about Moses, maybe, but it is his FAITH applied there and then. Not that Moses didn't have to apply his "own-faith" and ask GOD to "Show me your Glory" (Exodus 33:12). Our LORD says, "When my GLORY passes by (not IF), I, your GOD, will put YOU in a CLEFT in the ROCK (that's ME), and I have COVERED you with my HAND until I hath PASSED BY!!!!" So, the LORD tucked Moses into the ROCKS and passed.

Where are the STORMS of Our Life? Why are we confronted? Write it, sing it—what Our God has REVEALED in and through Us—that FAITH, GIVEN in Romans 12:3, to EVERYONE OF US, hath shown in Us. AMEN!!!"**

IN DANIEL 3, the three Hebrew boys — **Shadrach, Meshach, and Abednego** — were assigned by **King Nebuchadnezzar** to the fire! But what? They said, **"We will not bow to anything but our faith!!"**

I want us to open our eyes again — their faith was planted in them, **100%**, as even if death pays us a visit, **our faith is our shield.**

And please note, it was **after** they exposed their faith — yes, **after**, not before — that a **fourth person showed up!**
Amen! Hallelujah!!!

Isaac taken to the back of the mountain. Where was the **shepherd-boy???**

The Woman with the Issue of Blood wanted to touch the **hem of God's robe (garment) — why?**
She had **faith**, but from where did she **get it?**

If we allow the **Spirit** to reside (live) in us — what, and whose action, will we really be living in?

Galatians 5:13 — We have been called into **liberty** (i.e. being free in society from oppressive limits imposed by authority).
Galatians 5:1 — Christ has set us free!

Faith is built on **rock**, as He said unto Peter,

"Upon this rock I will build..."

What?

The songwriter confirms it:

"On Christ, the solid Rock, we stand —
Not sand that easily washes away!"

1 Chronicles 4:9–10 — *"And Jabez was more honorable than his brothers; and his mother called his name Jabez, saying, 'Because I bare him in sorrow.'"*

She did not realize that **one's birth never determines one's destination!**

In verse 10, we see what **faith** in Jabez allowed him to declare before the God of Israel:

"Oh, that Thou wouldest bless me indeed, and enlarge my border, and that Thine hand might be with me, and that Thou wouldest keep me from evil, that it may not grieve me!"

That is **total boldness — the kind that activates faith!**
And yes, **God granted Jabez all that he asked for** — every wish, every heart's desire, because his faith spoke louder than his circumstance.

Isaiah 53:5

"They are calling a nation they do not know, and nations that do not know them shall run to thee, because the Lord thy God hath glorified thee."

Here, we see the unfolding of divine connection — people drawn not by recognition, but by **revelation**. A nation runs toward another *because God has glorified it*. This is the power of faith in motion —

faith that qualifies us to walk into paths we've never known, both **physically and spiritually.**

Faith pushes us beyond familiarity. It leads us into the unseen, the untraveled, the unexpected. It calls us to believe before we see, to trust when the map is blank.

1. God's Ways Are Beyond Ours

Isaiah 55:8 reminds us:

"For My thoughts are not your thoughts, neither are your ways My ways," saith the Lord.

Just as the heavens are higher than the earth, so are His thoughts higher than ours. This is not distance—it is **divine distinction**. God's mind operates in eternity; ours struggles in time.

When we cannot trace His hand, we are invited to **trust His heart.**

2. The Myrtle Tree – A Symbol of Hope and Renewal

Referenced in **Isaiah 55:13** and **Zechariah 1:8**, the *Myrtle Tree* represents:

- **Hope** in desolation
- **Purity** through trial
- **Rebirth** through restoration

In Zechariah's vision, the Lord stands among the myrtle trees, a sign that **God dwells among His humble people** — those being renewed in faith. The myrtle grows low yet fragrant; it blooms even in shadow. So too, faith grows in hidden places — unseen but unshaken.

3. Faith and Trust – A Divine Partnership

Faith without trust is incomplete.
Faith believes God *can.*
Trust rests knowing God *will.*

To understand trust, let's look at something familiar — the **Trust Fund**.
We deposit our money into an institution because we believe in its reliability and track record. We trust that our investment will yield a secure return.

Now, apply that to your relationship with God.
He invites us to deposit not just money, but **our very lives** into His divine *Trust Bank*. The Lord Himself is our "Trust Fund." His *Word* is our investment document. His *Spirit* is the divine banker who guarantees eternal return — **new life, peace, and everlasting joy.**

4. Faith Matures Through Process

Consider Joseph — from the **pit to the palace**.
Consider Jesus — from the **manger to the cross**.

Each journey was filled with trials, misunderstandings, betrayal, and waiting — but also faith that **the vision would come to pass.**

Habakkuk 1:2 cries,

"O Lord, how long shall I cry, and thou wilt not hear? Even cry out unto thee of violence, and thou wilt not save?"

But **Habakkuk 2:3** answers with power:

"For the vision is yet for an appointed time... though it tarry, wait for it; it shall surely come, it will not tarry."

Faith is not delayed—it's *developing*.
While we wait, God works.

5. The Engine of Faith

Faith operates like a car.

- **Hope** gets us in the vehicle.
- **The Word** puts the key in our hand.
- **Trust** starts the ignition.
- **Faith** shifts it into gear.

Then, we move — not by sight, but by belief.

When faith is active, even in stillness, we are going somewhere.
When faith is growing, even in waiting, we are progressing.
When faith is planted, even in darkness, we are rising.

Hallelujah! Faith drives the impossible into reality.

6. The Divine Return on Investment

Every act of trust is a **spiritual deposit**.
Every prayer, every tear, every "yes, Lord" earns eternal interest in Heaven's treasury.

Just as earthly banks guarantee a rate of return, God guarantees **abundant life** — not always in the same currency we expect, but always in the fullness of His promise.

"He who began a good work in you will perform it until the day of Christ Jesus."
— Philippians 1:6

Closing Reflection

Faith is the engine.
Trust is the steering wheel.
Hope is the key.
The Word is the fuel.
And grace — grace is the road that never ends.

So, keep driving. Keep trusting. Keep sowing.

Your divine returns are already in motion — *for the vision is for an appointed time, and it shall surely come!*

Hallelujah!

Chapter 4

SO, WE HAVE THE FAITH ACCELERATOR "PEDAL" ... SO PRESS ON IT!!!

And you will never get a ticket for "over-speeding."

Let's take a look at ACTS 10 **v.48** — "They then prayed for him to tarry certain days."

The **power of prayer** is the **strength of faith.**

The **attack** that will come... this attack is a hostile act, a vicious act, and there are many reasons why they come!
(Job 1:1–9; Job 2:2 and v.6)

Here Job lost his riches — all of it — but what did Job not lose? **His faith.** He never lost it.

Can I send you to battle without training? **No, I cannot!**

So, as My child, know that faith is born not just in you, but that it is the natural ingredient given. So, I must trust you just as I trusted Adam, Cain, Mary, and Moses!!!

Do not get too comfortable, My child, but I will allow — not send — people around you (friends, family, Christians, pastors, church brothers) to be the ones who attack you!!!

Why would You do that, Lord?

"I want to be holy!!"

A prophet who rebelled against God and fled from His commands ended up in the **belly of a whale** on his way to **Nineveh**, a wicked city in Iraq.

In *Acts 9*, Saul, on his Damascus Road, **fell to the ground** — a turning point of transformation.

James 2:26 reminds us:

"Faith without works (action) is dead."

What happens here is this: **we are spiritually dead**, as if we are not saved.

Look at our car without its battery — what happens?
It will never start!
That's **us without faith** — we cannot and will not please God.

If we commit adultery, we sin — and that does not please God.
But when we have **no evidence of faith** in our life, we are **not pleasing in His sight!**

Faith Is Mandatory

Faith is **mandatory** in our life when we face uncertainty — to **navigate unknown situations** where outcomes are unclear.

When standing in adversity, we find comfort in faith — in times of:

- illness,
- loss,
- hardship,
- life-changing decisions (both long-term and short-term).

Faith is the **compass for direction** — it brings:

- a sense of belonging,
- the power to overcome fear and anxiety,
- reassurance, peace, and stability amid uncertainty,
- motivation,
- and renewal in times of doubt or crisis.

Let us ask ourselves:

"Where does faith come from?"

Faith and Reconciliation

Let's pause at *2 Corinthians 5:18*, which says:

"And all things are of God, who hath reconciled us to Himself, and hath given to us the ministry of reconciliation;

to wit (mental sharpness, inventiveness, keen intelligence), that God was in Christ, reconciling the world unto Himself;
and now we are ambassadors of Him, Christ!"

And further down, in verse 17:

"Come out from among them, and be ye separated, saith the Lord, and touch nothing unclean, and I will receive you."

This is **pronounced faith** imparted **to us and in us**.
We can truly say:

"Thank You, Father, for not leaving us in a place of no hope —
a place that could have separated us from You.
Thank You, Lord, for opening the way for us to come boldly to You.
Not only to You, Lord, but to those around us —
that we may be a witness and a minister to Your throne.
Lord, it's the faith planted in us that manifests boldly for restoration
—
all because of faith, both Yours and the one instilled in us.
Hallelujah!"

NOW, LET US LOOK AT FAITH AND THE ABILITY IN OBTAINING IT (FAITH)

The Lord says it: "Whatever we ask or request will come to us. Before you call or ask, I will answer" (**Isaiah 65:24**).

So, let us look at the comparison.

Firstly, the time I will need to go to the gym — months, years — a lot of time.
Next, monetary cost: $300, $5,000, $8,000? A huge sacrifice in time and money!!!
And results? Say I even lost thirty pounds.

Let us go into another lane and go to our "**Spiritual Gym**."
Wow!!!

In **Romans 12:3**, He, our God, has given each one of us our own measure of faith!

Really now, Lord? When Apostle preached that that Sunday, I was going to leave "his" church. As a child of God, I thought faith is what I work for — and a lot of work, a whole lot!!!

So, the time and cost at the gym we are spending? We have it already — just as we can see, hear, smell! Amen!

Crucify our doubts and resurrect what is already in us — faith!
And command those mountains to move — relocate!

Jabez says his name means poverty, but what am I going to do? Ignore that and use the faith planted in me, then use my eyes to see what God has already given me, before I was born (**Jeremiah**)! Amen!

Job 1:8 — And the Lord said to Satan, "Have you, the devil, considered my servant, my child Job?"

Job was very rich, wealthy, very prosperous on the face of the earth, and he, Job, feared God and was blameless!

Job lost his earthly riches, family, wealth, and his "friends" wanted him to "dry up." Some thought Job had sinned! But Job remained faithful — from You, his bank, his faith-bank!

And God built up Job through the trials to purity, to strengthen, and finally Job gained 1,000-fold restoration!

Our God is never short on what He has for us. It's the other way around — where we are of no faith, so we have not!!! Not God our Father!

Mike Tyson, a boxer, chose fighting as the physical way to express his lifestyle of where he was brought up, and someone saw that fighting and made him be a boxer. He had the basic ingredients.

It's just how we, as Christians, have the basic ingredient — faith — and it's for us to use it.
And we get it at church, Sunday school, and reading the Word.

He had boldness, confidence in his personal capabilities, and he had a trainer to bring out those capabilities. Amen!

So too are we. Our God sees and knows Peter's capabilities, just as He knows ours, and has planted faith in us to go in His name — like Jonah in the whale's belly.

We each have to do a search in our own self and see what we are to do.
Our Lord says we are to seek Him first — that takes our faith.
Then, after, all things will be added — takes faith!

One will ask: did Joseph know where his life was going to take him? No!
Did Mary know? No!
Do we know? No!
But we are to trust in Him, live in Him — and that is exactly what faith does — faith in action!

Pitfalls vs Pitstops
Jeremiah 1:5 — "Before I, the Lord, formed you, created you, I, the Lord, know you (from the beginning). And before you comest here on earth, Job, I, your God, know you; and I, your Lord, sanctified you, Job. I approved you, Job. I assigned you, Job. I ordained you, Job!"

And never forget this — walk with that, sleep with that — it is your GPS, your spiritual GPS!

This ordination means I, your God, have charged you, energized you as a prophet, not just to you here in (place/country), but to all nations!

Job has a tremendous assignment as a teenager, with purpose thrown unto him!
But isn't that a common thing God does?

Look at Paul in **Galatians 1:15** — "When it pleased God, He separated me from my mother's womb and called me by His grace!"

Why did God do this? God knows us, what He has built us with (faith), and what He has planted in us — faith!

I look at my five (5) children, and they carry some pronounced resemblance that they are my children — and this is an earthly matter. So why am I a God-child and do not have His DNA?
Why do I not "walk on water???"

Is it that I am holding onto fear — law of gravity?
Is it my "ears" I am depending on to "hear," or my "heart???"

How many times do my children "mimic" me — especially the boys — so why am I not able to do likewise of my God?

Let's peep over to Adam — he is created in God's own likeness and is given dominion. Is that the same given to us?

Where did God send Abraham? Abraham did not know two things:
1 Where he is to go — that's one.
2 Who (or what) will be the sacrifice?

Is Abraham exercising "something" he does not have?

There was no written Word; Abraham had no source but **Spirit to Spirit!!!!**

Come with me to **Matthew 11:15** — "He that hath ear to hear, let him, let her hear!!!"

Just as we open our heart, so too do we open our ear!

Isaiah 49:1 — Look where Isaiah's faith was born: "The Lord has, hath, called me from my mother's womb!"

Let us ask ourselves — has He called me? Yes or no?

And when did He? Before or after birth?

Matthew 22:14 — "Many are called, but few are chosen." (Jesus' parable.)

Not many invited guests turned up at the wedding. Why? They were "busy!!!"

We have an invitation — look good, check your memory!

Why do you have no faith? Been in "church" fifteen years — I pray, I witness, I go to Sabbath, I go to Sunday church, my mother sings on the choir, my father is the pastor, etc.

But when it comes to faith? I have none, and I am doing great!

Without faith, it is impossible to please God (**Hebrews 11:6**).

The option of faith?

He that cometh to our God must believe that — must know that our God is our rewarder unto our coming to Him! Hallelujah!!!

In **Daniel 6:22-23**, here is the full exposure of Daniel's faith, trust, and confidence in his faith that was planted by God.

Daniel says, "My God knew that I was innocent, and He, God, sent an angel to keep me."

Wow!!!

It is so awesome when we come full circle with Him living in us as we live in Him!!!

Jesus told them to re-do what they did before: "Cast your net in the water, but on this side."

Again, effort vs faith. Peter was using his own resources — effort — instead of faith. How often we do this!

Let's look in **Romans 3:24** — that we are justified, made in righteousness, freely by God's grace through Jesus Christ — all of this by faith!

Not by nationality, not by money, not by being married, not by being a university graduate — none of that!

As we, men, women, and children, are all justified by faith planted in all of us, we do not go by any deeds of the law (**Romans 3:28**).

Slipping down to **Romans 4:3** — "Abraham believed God, and that qualified him, Abraham, as righteous."

Now let's think — what happened here for Abraham?
That belief he had gave birth to what? Faith!!!

And Abraham, being not weak in faith, even at 100 years of age, never staggered on becoming a father!

Which one of us hides what power has been bestowed upon us, even greater than Solomon?
Yes, Solomon!

Did He not say, as God to us, that greater things will we do than He, the Son of God!

It's a baton passed on to us so we will relay Him and the power of faith given to us — our own measure (**Romans 12**).

Peter asked, "Lord, if it is You, bid me come!"
What did Peter actually do? Looked for identification — for who was he, and what level of power he had!

Luke 6:35 — "Love our enemies as Christ loves us." Faith in gear!
We are (to be like) Him!

Christ says, "When you see Me, Christ, you see who? The Father!"

Matthew 14 — "Bring them here to Me (God)" — fish and bread for 5,000 people — He then connected to His Father and then relayed unto who? Us!!!!!

"Let the mind of Christ be also in us" (**Philippians 2:5**).

Our year of Jubilee — our 50th year — a new beginning.
All past debts are cancelled.

It's my faith that turns on a switch that has power already.
The power, the electricity, is already in us from birth — so we are the light, the bulb, that beams God's power in us through faith!

When your boss asks you, "When are you coming to work?" you say, without thinking, "Monday!" And you wonder why?

I want us to get to the same point when we ask ourselves, "When will I get my salary increase?" — and be bold to give an answer!

I want to gain muscles, so I build muscles — I exercise appropriately, exercising specific exercises that will do just that.

What's the difference in building my faith?

Romans 12:3 says it all — look it up, I will wait. Make sure you get it.

Go to our **Spiritual Gym!**

Lift your faith muscles — 1, 2, 3, 4, 5, 6! Amen!!!

- Capitalized divine pronouns and scriptural references for consistency.

- **"WHAT PROOF DO I HAVE THAT I HAVE FAITH?**
  (HEB 11 vs 1–16) Not much help to think I have FAITH in me, much more to think it has been already given to me! Let me look back at how I was CONCEIVED, how we were CONCEIVED—we all were CONCEIVED IN SIN, SHAPED in INIQUITY.

- (v2) Look at ABRAHAM, Our Father (Father of all Nations), through which we receive IMPLICIT, STRONG FAITH! Out of Our RECREATED SPIRIT is WHERE FAITH is ACTIVATED (Heb 11), and this is what LAUNCHES OUR WORSHIP! It is our FAITH-SWITCH!

- DAVID, in Psalm 27:4, reminds ME, US... when troubles come, Lord, YOU are MY HELP; yes, YOU sure RESCUE ME again and again! Please remember FAITH is PLANTED in YOU, and in ME—yes, it is the SUBSTANCE we have that BRINGS OUT our HOPE into REALITY.

- Peter had hope when HE asked JESUS to bid him come; so too is the FAITH in that Wife that says, "until death do us PART!" That statement is solidified when we take our water baptism.

- FAITH is Our SPIRITUAL, HEAVENLY CURRENCY that is given to US here on EARTH to do "all things, greater THINGS than I, the Son of GOD!" Stare at HIS WORDS when HE says, "Before we were CONCEIVED in our Mothers' WOMB, I knew YOU."

- These TWO words can be neighbors depending on where YOU, WE choose to place them. They can get to the point where they do not know each other!!! Did the Bible say, "HE WHO KNEW NO SIN...?" As we see in 2 Corinthians 5:21, so WE—YES, WE—are MADE Righteousness of HIM, of GOD!!! The same thing ABRAHAM "aspires" for.

- What WEIGHT are we carrying, and how LONG are we carrying this WEIGHT? Let US stop at Chapter 4 in the same HEBREWS, in verse 12 (PAGE 35):
"MY POWERFUL WORD IS SHARP AS A SURGEON'S SCALPEL, CUTTING THROUGH EVERYTHING, WHETHER DOUBT OR DEFENCE, LAYING US OPEN TO LISTEN, AND TO OBEY!"

- This is a HEART-BYPASS driving into FAITH-CITY, and this is our RESIDENTIAL ADDRESS!

- We are fully protected by GOD through GRACE, which is the UMBRELLA that shields and covers the gift of FAITH planted in US. And that FAITH is **the** GIFT—not **a** gift—that Our LORD GOD looks at and is PLEASED!

- And just as we put on the WHOLE ARMOUR of GOD, it is FAITH that allows that DRESSING! Ask DAVID about that when He was up against GOLIATH—or the woman, a prostitute, at the pool!"

Chapter 5

The tree of our faith God planted in our garden, just like Adam's Garden of Eden.
But here He said,

"From this tree only should you eat, as all others you will fail."

God tells us that this **Tree of Faith** planted here goes in **two directions** — one goes **up**, and the other goes **down**.
Mary, Paul, Carmen, Lionell!

And of course, He says,

"I have given you branches and leaves that the world will see and be able to identify who you really are."

My children, you grow **bidirectional** — the *up-and-down* system you have inherited from Me, your God and Father.

This **bidirectional growth** you are made in — one that goes **upward** — is called **phototropic** (biofilms), and the other that goes **downward** is called **gravitropic**.

My children, they grow in opposite directions but remain the **same tree**, the **same plant**, and **bear the same fruit** of Me, who planted it in My garden!

You are assigned to live in accordance with Me who planted you, for that is **why I made you!**

The Gravitropic Growth

Let me start with **gravitropic growth**, as this is what creates the other growth.

As the tree you are, you grow **away from light**, just as I, Jesus, went to the grave — and so does the plant.

It is a coordinated process of **differential growth** by a plant in response to gravity — both **natural and artificial**.

Now we are watered by the **Holy Spirit**, and let us realize that just as we water our plants,

it is not the water the plants want,
but the water softens the soil for the plant to send its roots deeper and further.
Amen!

Rooted in Him

"Rooted and built up in Him, and established in the faith, as ye have been taught."
— **Colossians 2:7**

So, **faith is at the inception of Adam and Eve**, as the devil knew they would not die physically but become spiritual!

Why?
Their **faith was shattered**!

The devil always goes after our **faith**.
And again, the Lord says,

"Without faith it is impossible to please God."

Yes — our same God says that **when we have no faith, we cannot please Him.**

Did God, through Jesus, go into *the earth*?
Yes, He did!

Let us make a stop here and fill up our tank.
God says,

"I am with you always."

So how am I *not* pleasing in His sight?
That is a great question — and one I cannot answer myself!

Let's pray about it…

He says He is **omnipresent**, yes?
So, He will hear — surely!

But will He answer?

And if He does — what will it be?

What *you* want to hear? Or what *He* says?

"He that has an ear, let him hear what the Lord says."

The **root system** of our life in faith grows **away from light**, into **deeper darkness**, and it builds **deep roots** — spreading and strengthening our foundation in faith.

So when we are about to reach our **phototropic status**, showing exactly who we are, we already have a **preset foundation**.

Amen!

"We must be able to identify our pitfalls, different from our pitstops!"

(Jeremiah 1:5) — "Before I, the LORD, formed and created thee in the womb, I knew (not *know*) thee; and before thou camest forth out of the womb, I sanctified thee (approved) and ordained thee (charged with holy orders) — just as I came in Mary's womb!"

When was Jeremiah called a prophet unto the nations? How long did Jeremiah have to labor? Did we realize that Jeremiah had **two wombs**?

(Luke 12:32) — "Fear not, my little flock, for it is your Father's pleasure to give you, my Kingdom."

Trust Me — I give you My only Son *(Romans 8:32)* — delivered Him up for you all, and I freely give unto you, My children, **all things… all things!**

So, let us turn on our **"Faith Switch"** and see the **fullness of My faith** planted within you!

Building Faith — Even in the Birds and the Bats

Even the **bats** teach us about **faith**.
They fly only at **night** — and though they **cannot see**, they still soar with confidence.
They weigh less than an ounce, as light as a pencil, yet they eat up to their **own body weight** in insects — mosquitoes, beetles, and bugs.

These tiny creatures save farmers an estimated **$3 billion** each year in insect control.
How? By using the system **God Himself designed** — they send out **echolocation sounds** to find food and avoid obstacles.

They trust completely in what God gave them.
That is **faith** — faith in the unseen, faith in the Creator's perfect system.

1. Give Ear — Not Ears

God says, *"Give ear,"* not *ears*. Why? Because He wants our **attention**, not just our hearing. He desires our **whole being** tuned to

His voice — spirit, soul, and heart united.
This is not a casual invitation. It is a **command**: *"Come to Me."*

Who is calling?
It is the **Lord Himself**, saying, *"Hear Me, that your soul may live."*

Rockets after early take-off (60–90 minutes), it releases a heavy portion of its weight at a certain altitude. **Why?**

We are to **lay aside the things (weight), sins that so easily beset us**, and **run, walk, drive** (Hebrews 12:1).

Procrastination, disobedience, slow motion — these are the **weights** we are to get rid of so **faith will come and reside in us**.

Please do not miss it — **GOD has (past tense) given us our faith from day one!**

Jeremiah, a teenager, was assigned to ministry, but **Jeremiah tried to refuse his assignment**. He was looking at what? **His age.**
While GOD was looking at what? **His heart!**

It is out of the **abundance of the heart** our **mouth speaks, Hallelujah!**

We ask ourselves — **is my faith door locked? Shut? Or closed?**

Our God knows **when to open doors**, and **He knows when to close them**.

It is for us to know **when to enter** and **when to close**.

Be careful — as most doors **swing both ways**.

Be **very careful**, our **faith-door** swings **one way only!**

Fill me up, to overflow, so this child really begins to run over anything not of You, Lord. **Amen!!!**

As we **land**, we see how well we have **enjoyed our flight in faith** (title of my first book) and are **landing with faith. Amen!**

As we disembark, remember **Psalm 91:1** — that we are now dwelling in His secret place of our Most High God.

Therefore, we live under His shadows, and we must keep reminding ourselves — He, God, is our **Fortress**, and that is where our **Trust** resides.

So, the afflictions that will try to confront me —

"My Lord delivered us from them all." *(Psalm 34:19)*

And, my friends, walk boldly and smile as you see the **1,000 on the ground on your right** and the **10,000 on your left side** — none will come near to us, none!

1 John 4:4 clearly tells us who we are:

"God's little children, in whom God lives."

Hallelujah!

And Lord, we thank You for Your decree that established unto us to walk in that light that shows us the way preset before us. **Amen! Hallelujah!**

As we walk through "**customs**" and are welcomed by "**family**," many people smiling with us — we recognize that we really were lifted up from this "earth," and people are **coming to us**, as in the **John 12:32 experience. Hallelujah!**

And we feel this change — pleasant and reassuring — as finally we are **strong in You, Lord,** and feel the full power of You might, wearing Your whole armour that allows us to stand in the liberty with which You have set us!

Thank You, Lord!

And as we go to collect our bags…
and pay our duty…

"We must be able to identify our pitfalls, different from our pitstops!"

(Jeremiah 1:5) — "Before I, the LORD, formed and created thee in the womb, I knew (not *know*) thee; and before thou camest forth out

of the womb, I sanctified thee (approved) and ordained thee (charged with holy orders) — just as I came in Mary's womb!"

When was Jeremiah called a prophet unto the nations? How long did Jeremiah have to labor? Did we realize that Jeremiah had **two wombs**?

(Luke 12:32) — "Fear not, my little flock, for it is your Father's pleasure to give you my Kingdom."

Trust Me — I give you My only Son *(Romans 8:32)* — delivered Him up for you all, and I freely give unto you, My children, **all things... all things!**

So, let us turn on our **"Faith Switch"** and see the **fullness of My faith** planted within you!

Matthew 5:44 – *Faith has no sleeping room in the House of Faith (HOF).*
It must be in the **"gym"** — always in **gear**, **exercising** (for faith without works is dead).
We are faced with this **command**:

"Love my (our) enemies and pray for them that persecute me."

Matthew 5:46 asks us clearly:
If we love those who love us, then there is **no evidence of faith**.
And no faith means?

We can never **please God**, and we become **hypocrites** —
(and I didn't call you that; I would not do that — it is *the Word*).

When we reach that point, we are at the **table of unanswered prayers**,
and our **faith wires** become completely **disconnected!**

At this point, your **lights go out** — not dim, but **totally out!**
It's the same with FPL (the light company in the USA) or JPS (in Jamaica).
And when this happens, it comes with a **cost!**

The Prodigal Son Example

The **Prodigal Son**, what did he do?
He took his **portion** and said,

"Dad, I will not trust you anymore. I know that my faith is much better than yours, so give me my portion — now!"

This son had all the **faith**, **trust**, and **confidence** in **himself**, thinking he knew it all.
And many of us live this same way.

Because I am an **Accountant**, I thought I knew how to manage my finances —
and I **failed!**

Because I am a **Doctor**, I thought I could take care of my health — but I ended up in the **hospital**, dying!

The **Titanic** was made by engineers second to none — it was said to be unsinkable.
But it **did sink!**

Noah's Ark, on the other hand, was built by a **Carpenter** —
Did it sink? **No!**

The Scripture reminds us:

"Trust in the Lord and never lean to our own understanding."

Ephesians 6:12 reminds us:

"For we wrestle not against flesh and blood, but against principalities, powers, rulers of darkness, and spiritual wickedness in high places."

Our true battles are never against people — they are **spiritual**.
And so are our revelations.

Matthew 16:17 —

"Blessed art thou, Simon Barjona, for flesh and blood hath not revealed it unto thee, but My Father which is in Heaven."

Jesus made it clear — divine revelation comes only from **God**, not human understanding.

Then, in **Romans 8:38–39**, we are reminded of the unbreakable truth:

"Nothing can separate us from the love of God which is in Christ Jesus (note: Christ Jesus, the resurrected one, not merely Jesus Christ the man)."

Not **death**, not **life**, not **angels**, **demons**, **powers**, **height**, **depth**, **the present**, **the future**, nor anything else in all creation.

But there are things that **distance us** from walking closely with Him —

✝ **Unconfessed sin**
✝ **Pride**
✝ **Idolatry**
✝ **Selfishness**
✝ **Good deeds done without love**
✝ **A lost sense of purpose**

Still, even when we falter, **God's love remains constant** — waiting for us to return, repent, and receive His revelation anew.

Testimony

I drove up to a supermarket to get a few items. And as I opened the door to come out, the LORD visited me — in my casual clothes — and said,
"My son, I am pleased with you."

And He repeated it ten times,
"Yes, I am pleased with you."

Why would GOD do that?
It is the level of relationship GOD allows us to have with Him!

I was at church and was doing Young Converts Class, and the LORD, through the Holy Spirit, led me to a tiny teenager, about fifteen.
And GOD gave me the prophecy that he will be a medical doctor.

His mother then confirmed and said that is all he aspires for — from the age of four!

This nurse, earning $500 per week, proudly gave her 10%, but the preacher picked her out of the crowd and quietly told her, "God says you must give $1,000 — two weeks' pay."

And she had just given her 10%! The preacher was from a visiting church.

So, the member called the treasurer on Monday — did not get her. She called the bank — it was paid already!

She was wondering what to do. "Okay," she thought, "I am going to get at least $10,000, maybe $100,000!"

But what did she get? $0.00.

'Give, and it shall be given back, pressed down and shaken over.' But that Scripture was not for me — because obedience is better than sacrifice.

Prophecy Received

"Look into your brown folder."
"I have granted you, My son — added years against your enemy."

You have been assigned to more preaching, to pick up your microphone and preach — even in unfamiliar places.

The Lord says:

"You are assigned much grace."

Remember Abraham — at *ninety-five years old*, he begat Isaac, the son of promise!
So shall it be with you — your latter glory shall be greater than the former.

This is a season of different preaching, a new anointing, a new sound — birthed through Rhema Word.

For what is *1 plus 1*?
It can be *2* — or it can be *22*!
Such is the mystery of God's divine multiplication and revelation.

Unconscious for **fourteen days** through alcohol in **Jamaica, October 1977** — they said, *"He will be a vegetable."*
But the Lord said,

"Go thy way and sin no more."
Easier said than done...

Then Came Another Call

November 2020, at **Carol's Home**, God called me again — this time with a **PCA Assignment.**
That's where **8100/214** was birthed — on a **Friday afternoon at 6 PM.**

Fast forward to **November 2024** — the same God who called me then, took my **$10,000 (from June 2024)** and turned it into **$300,000!**
From *zero ($30K)* to *100 mph ($300K)* — in less than **thirty seconds!**

The Song That Defines the Journey

🎵 *"Victory Belongs to Jesus"* by **Todd Dulaney**
The song declares:

"Victory belongs to who?"
"Victory belongs to Jesus."

Victory over what? Over **sin**, over **shame**, over **death**, over **every chain** that tried to bind me.

Who challenges **Jesus**?
No one.
Who challenges **me**?
Those who challenge the Jesus **in me.**

Because I am not Jesus — but **He lives in me!**
And in every challenge, He whispers:

"Stand still and see the salvation of the Lord."

He, GOD, says:

"Come, approach boldly, without fear, to My throne of grace." — **Hebrews 4:16** That is the practical and spiritual exercise of exposing our faith, already given in **Romans 12:1–6**

Songs of Prescription

1. COME JESUS COME BY CECE WINANS
2. SOMETIMES IT TAKES A MOUNTAIN BY GAITER BAND
3. LORD DO IT FOR ME BY ZACARDI CORTEZ
4. PSALM 23 I AM NOT ALONE BY SCRIPTURE MEDITATIONS

THE HOLY SPIRIT PRESCRIPTION

5. THE MASTER'S CALLING BY DEBORAH JOY
6. I GIVE MYSELF AWAY BY WILLIAM MCDOWELL
7. HOW MANY TIMES BY BRROKLYN TABERNACLE
8. LORD HELP ME BY CECE WINANS.

THE VICTORY LAP

9. YOU DESERVE THE GLORY BY JOSUE AVILA
10. NO ORDINARYSERVANT BY KELANTAE GAVIN
11. FOR GOD SO LOVE BY TASHA COBBS
12. HOLY SPIRIT YOU BY HEAVENS MATAMBIRA.

Thirty-Day Faith Scripture Plan

THE THIRTY BIBLE VERSES ON FAITH
(This goes where the 30-day Bible verses are.)

What we are to do is assign one verse per day, with a total focus on building on my strength in faith — not my weakness.

We will keep going to our "spiritual gym" to build our "faith muscle," so we will walk "on the water" as Moses did, and so did David, killing Goliath.

And do we not have "our own Goliath?"

Day 1 – Philippians 2:5
Let this mind be in you, which was also in Christ Jesus.

Day 2 – John 1:32
And John bare record, saying, "I saw the Spirit descending from Heaven like a dove, and it abode upon Him."

Day 3 – John 9:3
Jesus answered, "Neither hath this man sinned, nor his parents, but that the works of God should be made manifest in him."
(Blind from birth — Jesus told him to go to the pool of Siloam and wash.)

Day 4 – John 4:32

But He said unto them, His disciples, "I have meat to eat that ye know not of."

Day 5 – John 4:14

Jesus answered and said unto her, "Whosoever shall drink of this water that I give shall never thirst again; it shall be a well of water springing up into everlasting life."

Day 6 – Hebrews 2:6-7

What is man, that Thou art mindful of him? Or the Son of man, that Thou visitest him?
Thou madest him a little lower than the angels; Thou crownedst him with glory and honor, and didst set him over the works of Thy hands.

Day 7 – Luke 4:4

And Jesus answered, saying, "It is written, that man shall not live by bread alone, but by every word of God."

Day 8 – Psalm 27

Hold on to God's unchanging hand.

Day 9 – Romans 8:35

(Strongholds)

Day 10 – Isaiah 41:13

The Lord will hold our right hand.

Day 11 – Isaiah 40:31

They that wait upon the Lord shall renew their strength; they shall mount up with wings as eagles; they shall run and not be weary; they shall walk and not faint.

Day 12 – Psalm 119:2

Blessed are they that keep His testimonies and seek Him with their whole heart.

Day 13 – Psalm 119:11

Thy Word have I hid in my heart, that I might not sin against Thee.

Day 14 – 2 Chronicles 20:2

And David took the crown of their king from off his head, and found it to weigh a talent of gold (30–130 lbs). There were precious stones in it, and it was set upon David's head. He brought also exceeding much spoil out of the city.

Page 50 – Day 15 – Isaiah 43:21

This people have I formed for Myself; they shall show forth My praise.

Day 16 – Psalm 2:8

Ask of Me, and I will give Thee the heathen for Thine inheritance, and the uttermost parts of the earth for Thy possession.

Day 17 – Psalm 7:8

The Lord shall judge the people: judge me, O Lord, according to my righteousness and according to mine integrity that is in me.

Day 18 – Psalm 126:1

When the Lord turned again the captivity of Zion, we were like them that dream.

Day 19 – 1 Corinthians 2:9

But as it is written, eye hath not seen, nor ear heard, neither have entered into the heart of man the things which God hath prepared for them that love Him.

Day 20 – Matthew 4:11

Then the devil — the serpent, the devourer — leaveth Him (Jesus).

Day 21 – Matthew 4:10

Then said Jesus unto him, "Get thee hence, Satan! For it is written: Thou shalt worship and serve only the Lord thy God."

Day 22 – 2 Peter 3:9

Our Lord and Savior is not slack concerning His promises, and not willing that any should perish, but that all should come to repentance.

Day 23 – Ephesians 6:10

Finally, like Job, be strong using our faith muscle — in the Lord and in the power of His might!

Day 24 – Ephesians 6:14

Stand therefore — this attack will come; expect it. Do not hide, but have your loins girded about with truth, His Word, the Holy Spirit.

Day 25 – James 4:7
Resist the devil, put up that fight, and watch the devil flee from us, God's children!

Day 26 – Philippians 1:6
"That He who began a good work in you will perfect it until the day of Christ Jesus."
We are confident of this through faith.
Note: It says **Christ Jesus** — why? Because *Jesus Christ* is the man; *Christ* is the resurrected power!

Day 27 – 2 Samuel 11
At the time when kings go to battle, David sent Joab and his servants, and they destroyed the children of Ammon — while David remained in Jerusalem.

Day 28 – Acts 17:28
For in You I live, and move, and have my being. Christ comes so near that we move from courtship into marriage — and begin bearing fruit!

Day 29 – Romans 8:38-39
For I am persuaded that neither death, nor life, nor angels, nor principalities, nor powers, nor things present nor to come, nor height nor depth, nor any other creature, shall be able to separate us from the love of God, which is in Christ Jesus our Lord.

Day 30 – Ephesians 6:12
For we wrestle not against flesh and blood, but against principalities,

against powers, against the rulers of the darkness of this world, and against spiritual wickedness in high places. Therefore, put on the whole armor of God, with your loins girded in truth.

www.ingramcontent.com/pod-product-compliance
Lightning Source LLC
Chambersburg PA
CBHW051202120626
46547CB00012B/1164